C0-AUT-545

Any opinions within the Trust Equation are those of George Jackson or others quoted and not necessarily those of RJFS or Raymond James. Expressions of opinion are as of the publishing date and are subject to change without notice. The Trust Equation is not endorsed or promoted by RJFS or Raymond James. The information has been obtained from sources considered to be reliable, but we do not guarantee that the foregoing material is accurate or complete. Any information is not a complete summary or statement of all available data necessary for making an investment decision and does not constitute a recommendation. You should discuss any tax or legal matters with the appropriate professional. Case studies described are not representative of the experiences of all investors and do not offer any guarantee similar results will be achieved. Keep in mind that there is no assurance strategies like "trend investing" will ultimately be successful or profitable nor protect against a loss. Strategies and examples given may not be suitable for all investors. You should discuss your personal situation with a professional before investing.

George Jackson's services of financial, retirement and investment planning are offered exclusively through Raymond James Financial Services, Inc. Mr. Jackson is owner and president of Jackson Retirement Planning, Inc. Jackson Retirement Planning, Inc. is an independent firm not registered to offer securities or investment services. Mr. Jackson is a registered representative offering securities and investment advisory services through Raymond James Financial Services, Inc. Member NASD/SIPC located at 1515 International Parkway, Suite 1013 Heathrow, Florida 32746, 407-585-0235.

The Trust Equation

◆◆◆

The Savvy Investor's Guide to Selecting
A Competent, Ethical Financial Advisor

Steven Drozdeck ◆ Lyn Fisher

Copies of this book are available for purchase through:

Fisher LeBlanc Group
http://www.fisherleblanc.com
(435) 787-2900

Financial Forum Bookstore
http://www.ffbookstore.com
(435) 750-0062

Discounts available for volume purchases.

Publisher
Financial Forum Publishing
(435) 750-0062

The Trust Equation

Table of Contents

The Trust Equation

Foreword

The people you go to for advice – including financial advice – have a major impact on your future. Many people don't want to believe this initially, but then quickly realize it is absolutely true. You cannot do it all yourself; no one individual has all of the knowledge to survive and thrive in our complex world. In our interdependent society, you must rely on the knowledge and skills of certain key professionals – who, in turn, rely on a team – to provide you with the information you need to make informed decisions.

The question then becomes: Whom do you choose? Many people choose a friend or a friend of a friend because of the existing relationship. Unfortunately, this selection method is often woefully inadequate. The stories of people who became financially devastated because they trusted the wrong people are too numerous to mention. Acting on ill-conceived plans based on inadequate or incorrect information from incompetent individuals, is the harbinger of disaster.

If you were president of a major business, you would undoubtedly hire the best people available to you. Some of them might be friends, but friendship would not be the primary factor in the hiring process. You would hire people based on trust, competence, and their ability to fill a needed niche within your company. You would hold them accountable to certain standards, have periodic meetings, and expect them to meet or exceed your expectations. Similarly, as president/CEO of your personal financial entity, the same rigorous processes ought to be in place when choosing and working with financial professionals, including a financial advisor. After all, it is their advice that you will rely on, and it is *your* future that is at stake.

Your ability to identify and work with competent, high-level advisors is vital to your financial success. As you realize, not all financial advisors or financial firms are created equal. To assist you in selecting and evaluating a financial advisor and/or team, this book discusses:

- the important differences between advisors and their teams,
- what you should look for, expect and demand in terms of service,
- how you can evaluate an advisor,
- and how top advisors work with clients.

The 12 advisors interviewed for this book are quite willing to be evaluated against their competitors. High-level advisors welcome scrutiny from clients, attorneys, CPAs, and others because they show themselves to be demonstrably superior to the vast majority of competitors.

It's a Matter of Trust

Trust does not happen immediately or accidentally. It is usually based on certain objective and subjective "proofs" that, cumulatively, bring you to the decision that a person is trustworthy or reliable. While many people say they are trustworthy, loyal, helpful, friendly, courteous, kind, obedient, cheerful, thrifty, brave, clean, and reverent[1], we unfortunately have learned not to take everyone at face value. While we hope that people we rely on will be worthy of trust, they must prove their worthiness.

Children trust easily. As soon as they share a piece of candy, play together on the playground, walk together in line, or smile at one another, children become friends. Adults are more hesitant. We know it's not good to take everything at face value. We want to judge how we react to someone and how they react to us. We learn to trust someone who really understands our needs and tries to help whenever possible. That someone should complement our abilities, reduce our weaknesses, and enhance our strengths. And, that person should fit well into other aspects of our lives.

As an investor, you can do a number of things to help ensure that the advisor you pick to provide a high-level, comprehensive financial plan and/or manage some or all of your money is the right person for you. These things include:

- knowing what personal and financial objectives you wish to achieve,
- getting referrals for a financial advisor from other trusted professionals,
- checking on references provided by the advisor,
- asking astute questions and listening to the answers carefully,
- and allowing the advisor the time needed to produce results.

All of these things, plus more, are part of a mental equation that allows us to judge the trustworthiness of an advisor. We have helped quantify some of the elements of trust by examining several key concepts. With the help of 12 high-level financial advisors, we explore concepts such as business practices, the need for integrity, professional development, and teamwork. These advisors are industry leaders and models for discerning clients as well as other advisors.

Regardless of their years in the financial services business, they share common traits, including a commitment to excellence, a desire to help their clients fulfill their goals, and a high level of integrity. Most importantly, they really care about their clients.

Each chapter explores a different aspect of the trust equation and allows you to more fully understand the role of an advisor and what your current advisor is or isn't doing for you. *The Trust Equation* is more than a book on trust and integrity; it is about the people and businesses that exemplify these key traits.

◆◆◆

[1] The ideals promoted by the Boy Scouts of America

Chapter 1

The Five Continuums of Trust

There are well over one million people in the United States alone who call themselves financial advisors—people theoretically able to provide expert counsel on numerous money matters. Unfortunately, many are little more than financial salespeople who have only slightly more knowledge of their product or service than their clients or customers.

As stated in the foreward, you are President/CEO of your own financial firm and have a responsibility to choose competent, ethical, reliable professional advisors from many different fields. If you are successful in finding the right people, you will significantly increase the probability of realizing your dreams. If you fail to find the right group of people, you will most likely end up with a hodgepodge of investments that, at best, will produce mediocre results. In other words, the right people will help you put your financial house in order; the wrong people will create disarray.

Within this book you'll learn about the practices of high-level experts who serve as models that others aspire to be within the financial services field. You'll learn how to find good advisors, what questions to ask, and what differentiates their practices from their competitors. You'll find many other tools and ideas that can help you find competent, caring professionals.

The first tool is a method of looking at professionals from a different perspective than you may be used to. It will help you identify and determine what you want from a professional relationship.

The Five Continuums of Trust

The following five continuums will help you determine what you want from a professional relationship.

1. Education/knowledge
2. Advice
3. Compensation
4. Capabilities
5. Caring

Each is measured on a 10-scale value continuum. From this you can judge advisors in such key areas as skills, education, and service. (Note: This trust scale can be easily adapted to any professional or service provider.)

To start, mark on the table below how you feel the professionals in your life should rate. If you are like most people, you will want to rate them between 7 and 10.

Trust Continuum	"My advisor should rate..."									
Attribute/Characteristic	Low									High
1. Level of education / knowledge	1	2	3	4	5	6	7	8	9	10
2. Quality of professional advice	1	2	3	4	5	6	7	8	9	10
3. Fairness of fees charged	1	2	3	4	5	6	7	8	9	10
4. Personal and team capabilities	1	2	3	4	5	6	7	8	9	10
5. Degree of caring about clients	1	2	3	4	5	6	7	8	9	10

As you read the descriptions that follow, you can again determine the rating levels of the various professionals in your life – both financial and non-financial. You'll be rating the individual professional and/or team.

Education/Knowledge Continuum: It is very easy to obtain and learn the information needed to sell most financial products, such as stocks, bonds, mutual funds, insurance, etc. Far too often, the formal part of the educational process stops when the required product sales licenses are obtained. Such advisors obtain additional knowledge by reading sales-oriented literature and through "the school of hard knocks." When selecting an advisor, his or her level of personal experience should be one of your primary concerns. Ask yourself the question, "Do I want an advisor with a lot of experience or one who will be using me to gain experience for the future?"

In virtually all endeavors, a person's level of knowledge is directly proportional to his or her level of proficiency. Attaining knowledge is a lifelong activity that involves ongoing professional development using numerous avenues, all involving a tremendous amount of reading and study. All the advisors in this book spend a significant amount of time increasing their knowledge to better help clients achieve their goals.

Cella Quinn, President/CEO of Cella Quinn Investment Services[1] (Omaha, NE), adds that she enjoys the mental challenge of helping people build wealth and accomplish their dreams. "Building wealth for people is the most intellectual thing I can think of. After 33 years (of being in the investment arena), it's still a wonderful challenge."

Every person learns in a different way. Most advisors attend numerous industry conferences to update their skills. They read an extensive number of professional investment journals to constantly hone their knowledge and sophistication levels.

Knowledge is important, and Chris Doughty, Co-founder of ReAct! Group and First Vice President of Ziegler Investment Services Group (Milwaukee, WI), sagely observes that "wisdom" is what differentiates the good from the very best. Says Chris, "This is one of the only industries where you get better as you get older. Every single day you have the ability to learn something new or fine-tune a process. This (the financial services industry) isn't about being a young man's game. It's about wisdom and putting that wisdom to work."

He further comments on how many financial advisors don't accumulate wisdom but accumulate experience while making variations of the same mistake over and over again. One of the reasons for this, he says, is that such people are merely looking for answers on a day-to-day basis. "Wisdom doesn't come that way. It comes from discernment (and recognition) of the bigger picture."

Chris correctly notes that there is a huge difference between high-level professionals and the vast majority of financial sales representatives[2].

In our estimation, a large percentage of all financial representatives have minimal industry knowledge. This may seem a harsh statement, but

[1] Securities offered through Advantage Capital Corporation. A registered broker/dealer, NASD/SIPC.

[2] A note on nomenclature. We use the traditional term "financial representative" when referring to financial products or services salespeople at various banks, brokerage firms, and insurance companies. A variety of other titles are used by financial firms, including account executive, financial advisor, financial consultant, financial manager, financial practitioner, investment advisor/consultant/manager/practitioner/professional, bank-broker, bank investment/trust portfolio officer, agent, etc. Regardless of the title used, the vast majority of these people are paid to sell, and, hence, are financial product salespeople.

The terms financial advisor and high-level financial advisor are reserved in this book for individuals and teams that provide comprehensive financial advice and whose services go beyond the purchase or sale of stocks, bonds, mutual funds, insurance products, CDs, etc. they have attained numerous industry distinctions or extensive experience that help ensure that they have a substantially higher level of knowledge than most competitors.

it's true. It requires relatively little knowledge to pass financial licensing examinations. Financial representatives with less than three years of experience and who lack supplemental training usually fall on the lower end of the educational continuum. They often know only the bare basics and have only a bit more knowledge than their clients.

Financial representatives with five to 10 years in the business, and who have no supplemental training, often fall in the mid-range of the education/knowledge continuum. They've gathered quite a bit of information over the years and, hopefully, have learned through experience. However, without continuing education beyond the minimal industry requirements, they would probably rate in the 4 to 6 range on the education scale.

At the higher end of the spectrum are financial advisors who continually upgrade their knowledge through extensive reading and/or by attending industry conferences, thereby acquiring advanced information on financial services topics. Courses on insurance, financial planning, taxation, investment management, estate law and the like help ensure that they remain on the cutting edge of their professions.

Try this experiment. Ask your advisor to describe in detail what he or she does to stay on the cutting edge. What books or professional journals does he or she read? Can you borrow a copy of one of the journals? If you get vague answers, probe for specificity. If they can't be specific, then lower your education continuum rating.

Don't expect an advisor to be an expert on everything. That's just not possible. However, they or a team member should be an expert in the area(s) that impact you. For example, if you are retiring, seek out an advisor highly knowledgeable in retirement. If you want to fund a charitable enterprise, find someone with expertise in that area.

Your advisor should have a strong team of experts in other disciplines such as law, taxes, estate planning, etc., available for consultation. Ask who they work with and what their credentials are. (The Capabilities Continuum provides additional suggestions on this topic.)

Where is your advisor on the education/knowledge scale? (Be as objective as possible. Your wealth is at stake.)

Education/Knowledge Continuum Assessment	
Where is your advisor?	1 2 3 4 5 6 7 8 9 10
Where should he/she be?	1 2 3 4 5 6 7 8 9 10

Advice Continuum: Many people have received telephone calls from high-energy, persuasive promoters offering the latest "hot stock" that is going to double in the next few months. They only want "a commitment of a few thousand shares so you can get your feet wet." They make sales pitches without knowing anything about you except that you may have invested in the market before and that you probably have discretionary funds. Such people represent the extreme low-end of the advice continuum. While this approach may be okay for certain highly speculative and sophisticated investors, most people should avoid those "opportunities of a lifetime." This type of advisor usually makes no attempt to determine suitability, as required by the New York Stock exchange, and is only interested in making a sale. Avoid these people.

As you move up the advice continuum, you'll find the vast majority of advisors—those who offer a large array of financial products and services made available through their companies. However, many only ask you minimal information about your goals and objectives before making a recommendation. In general, the less the advisor knows about you, the more of a cookie-cutter solution you will receive. Be wary of the person who only asks the questions on a new account form and only concentrates on your financial status, as opposed to your overall needs.

Eric Hutchinson, CFP®, Chairman and CEO of Hutchinson/Ifrah Financial Services, Inc. (Little Rock, AR), notes that he started off as a traditional, commission-based stockbroker and was taught to call clients with a great story about how their lives would change (that is, they would make a lot of money) if they bought 10,000 shares of XYZ. Eric was very uncomfortable with recommending stocks to someone without knowing the big picture, and realized that he did not want to do business that way. He, like the other advisors within this book, strives to offer a substantially higher level of professionalism to clients.

Expanding on this point, Yale Levey, CFP® and Managing Director of Roseland Financial Group LLC[1] (Roseland, NJ), also made a decision to take his practice to a higher-level by taking a more diagnostic and holistic approach in working with clients. As a result, he transitioned to a more viable business model.

Looking back, Yale explains that a traditional broker uses a sales-driven, transactional approach while his practice, on the other hand, uses a more holistic, non-sales approach. "We listen to everything a prospect or client tells us. We listen to what their needs are as individuals, and then we take a diagnostic approach and make appropriate recommendations. While traditional brokers might say they do this, in actuality they probably don't. They are all about sales and commissions and not about implementing a comprehensive investment planning process. There's a big difference. Transactional businesses have a narrow focus, they are more shallow, while ours is more comprehensive, it's all encompassing. So from the client's perspective, our approach addresses more of their needs."

At the top of the advice continuum are advisors such as those inter-

[1] Securities offered through Royal Alliance Associates Inc. Member NASE/SIPC.

viewed for this book. They ask a more comprehensive set of questions, thereby gaining a better and broader understanding of a client's needs and objectives. Therefore, these advisors usually offer more customized solutions. The highest-level advisors won't make any recommendations until they have a thorough understanding of your financial needs and status. Furthermore, they will have an excellent understanding of your personal needs and goals, both short- and long-term. Their financial solutions are often the best crafted and most precisely tailored to your specific needs. They go far beyond the computer-generated financial planning solutions that are currently the rage at many firms.

These high-level advisors ask to see your tax returns, retirement plan documentation, complete portfolio, etc. Making a recommendation without having this information would be like a doctor prescribing medicine without conducting an examination. If an advisor doesn't ask to see, at the very least, your tax returns and similar information, question whether this person is right for you.

In addition, the highest-level advisors will explore lifestyle needs and legacy issues, asking questions such as:

- What values do you wish to pass on to your children, grandchildren, etc.?
- What differences do you wish to make for your church, community, country?
- If you could wave a magic wand and create the perfect lifestyle or existence for your family, what would it be like?
- What would you like to provide for your heirs?

Michael J. Searcy, ChFC, CFP®, AIF®, President, Searcy Financial Services, Inc. (Overland Park, KS) says he and his team ask their clients comprehensive questions about values and goals. They feel this differentiates them from their competitors because they spend the majority of their time, energy, and efforts helping clients identify and articulate their visions, commitments, and goals. "Most other advisors spend their time dealing with the things that we would consider 'commodities[1]' such as recommending and implementing the strategies, tools, and tactics used to carry out a (investment) plan," he says.

Advice Continuum Assessment										
Where is your advisor?	1	2	3	4	5	6	7	8	9	10
Where should he/she be?	1	2	3	4	5	6	7	8	9	10

Compensation Continuum: How does your financial advisor get paid? At one extreme is the majority of advisors who are paid purely on commission[2]. Yale Levey says commission-based financial advisors continually

[1] Commodities is a term referring to items or services that you can get almost anywhere.

[2] Commission: A service charge assessed by a broker or advisor in return for buying and selling securities.

face the situation of "If you aren't selling, you are starving."

Unless a commission-based advisor has a well-established practice, there may be a bias to sell you certain products. It is important to realize that commissions are not inherently self-serving or bad. Many experienced, well-established financial professionals earn enough commission income from multiple clients that they are somewhat insulated from the pressures to sell certain products and services. Many commission-based financial representatives are ethical and only recommend products and services they believe to be in your best interests. Additionally, many of the highest-level advisors receive commissions as one of their sources of compensation. It is also important to note that even salaried advisors may be pressured to generate more revenue. Always find out how the advisor and/or the firm make their money. They should be completely willing to discuss all fees involved and all sources of revenue.

At the other end of the scale are fee-only advisors who receive a fee based on the advice rendered; they do not receive any additional compensation from you or any other party when you implement their advice.

The term "fee-based" has a lot of different meanings. For example, a fee is charged for the creation of a financial plan. This may be a one-time fee and is usually determined by the complexity of the plan. If the advisor is managing your assets, you may be charged a percentage of the assets being managed on an annual basis. Compensation must always be weighed against the results produced and the services provided.

Some financial firms offer flat fees that may or may not be less than what you would have paid in commissions if you were charged for each separate transaction. Wrap accounts, where fees are bundled, are basically the same thing.

The important consideration is that an advisor provides full disclosure of fees and that all forms of compensation are shown to you. Ask yourself if your financial advisor made sure that you understood what you paid for and ensured that you were fully informed. (It's amazing how much people can pay in hidden fees.)

Eric Hutchinson explains, "Our clients are fine with us making a living. They're fine with paying us to do what we do best. They just want full disclosure. They want to understand what the costs are. They like fee-based compensation. Ultimately, we are able to structure the business so that the clients pay only one fee that covers everything we do for the them."

Compensation Continuum Assessment										
Where is your advisor?	1	2	3	4	5	6	7	8	9	10
Where should he/she be?	1	2	3	4	5	6	7	8	9	10

Capabilities Continuum: A high-level advisor provides a host of comprehensive services that cannot possibly be obtained from a traditional advisor working alone. The capabilities of a high-level advisor often include access to experts in different disciplines such as law, insurance, and taxes. On the other hand, the typical financial representative shares an administrative assistant (also known as a sales assistant or clerk) with three to five other advisors. This rep also has to wait in line to access experts within the firm – experts that the advisor probably has never met (or may never meet). These experts likely have only an academic knowledge of your needs and little, if any, concern about your investment outcome. After all, the outside experts are not part of an integrated team, don't have a personal relationship with the primary advisor, and usually are paid per case they handle – not for the value of their advice. Obviously, financial reps with limited resources should be ranked on the lower end of the capabilities continuum.

Of course, the lowest rating would go to an advisor who is a true lone wolf and who claims to know everything about investing. It might be wise to consider such people delusional and assign them a negative rating.

But how do you determine whether an advisor really has a team when everyone – even rookies – claims to have a complete team backing them? You should be able to find out the experts your advisor is relying upon. The advisor should have an in-depth and personal knowledge of these strategic partners and know their personal and professional backgrounds. You should be able to call that outside expert and ask about the abilities of your advisor. Basically, each should know the other well.

The advisors within this book have extensive networks of other professionals that they can rely upon.

Capabilities Continuum Assessment										
Where is your advisor?	1	2	3	4	5	6	7	8	9	10
Where should he/she be?	1	2	3	4	5	6	7	8	9	10

Caring Continuum: High-level advisors truly care about their clients like they would friends or family. Of course, everyone can say they care, regardless of whether they do or not. So, what is the proof that someone really cares? If you asked for references (and you should) as part of your personal due diligence, you should ask each reference questions such as:

- What does your team/advisor do that makes you a raving fan?
- Why did you choose him or her?
- How do you know they care?

Ask the advisor to describe a few situations in which he or she did something out of the ordinary for a client. (Additional questions will be suggested in a separate chapter.) For example, George Jackson, CPA[1], CFA, CFP®, CLU, ChFC, President of Jackson Retirement Planning, Inc. (Heathrow, FL), and his team regularly help their clients with personal matters even though they're not paid to do so. For example, they helped one client find an assisted living home, helped another sell their home, and even drove 150 miles to help another client sort through all her bills and prepare her income taxes.

Now that is showing true caring and concern.

Advisors can also demonstrate their "caring" by participating in and initiating community programs, helping with charitable foundations, sponsoring client appreciation events, and working with schools and children's programs. For example, Mike Piershale, principal at Piershale Financial Group with Raymond James Financial Services (McHenry, IL), took a leave of absence from his business in the early 1990s to run a bus ministry that brought 250 to 400 children from the poorest neighborhoods in Ponca City, Oklahoma to church functions. He devoted three years to that ministry and still actively supports a number of church-related activities for the needy.

A caring mentality should also exist not only within the teams and among the principals, but with all staff members, ranging from the receptionist to the executive assistant. When teams work together, socialize together, laugh together, and grow together, they create a caring environment. The staff compensation structure should also provide a win-win situation, not a situation of haves and have-nots. Caring is about setting up an organization in which each person's strengths are valued in a supportive, productive, and professional fashion.

Caring Continuum Assessment										
Where is your advisor?	1	2	3	4	5	6	7	8	9	10
Where should he/she be?	1	2	3	4	5	6	7	8	9	10

In Conclusion

You owe it to yourself to do what is necessary to choose the best advisors available to you. After all, it is your future that is at stake. When you take into consideration the five continuums, you will be able to make a more objective determination regarding an advisor's overall capabilities. If your advisor doesn't rank in the upper range of the assessment scale, ask yourself (and possibly them) how they compensate for their deficiencies.

Discuss with each potential or current advisor some of the questions suggested in the five continuums. Make sure you get answers that you like. If you don't, it's better to walk away now than be disappointed later.

◆◆◆

[1] Regulated by the state of Florida.

Hutchinson on Integrity

"Each member of our team is personally dedicated to our corporate vision of superior client service. With every contact, each client is made to feel special. It is clearly communicated that we care deeply about them as individuals and helping them achieve financial peace of mind.

The cold, indifferent, 'couldn't care less' attitudes often expressed by others in our society are the antithesis of the warm, caring, genuine interest communicated to our clients by every member of our team. Our approach to dealing with clients embodies a "win/win" philosophy and demonstrates traditional values of honesty, integrity, and the highest standards of professional ethics."

Eric Hutchinson, CFP®
Chairman & Chief Executive Officer
Hutchinson/Ifrah Financial Services, Inc.

Chapter 2

Solving the Trust Dilemma

Many financial advisors begin their careers working with individual clients and small businesses. No matter what type of firm these retail representatives might work for—bank, brokerage house, insurance company or international, national, regional, local—they usually sell products and services for a commission.

While they may give excellent financial advice, their livelihood depends on selling products, such as mutual funds, securities, bonds, and insurance. They don't necessarily get paid for their knowledge or abilities. Rather, they are paid when they have persuaded someone to purchase a product. This causes some clients to wonder about who actually benefits when a financial recommendation is made. Is there a conflict of interest?

As a result, many advisors have moved their businesses away from a pure commission-based structure to eliminate any potential conflict of interest. High-level advisors go to great lengths to ensure that any potential conflicts of interest are eliminated. Additionally, unless an advisor already has a well-established clientele, it becomes very difficult to service the client base because a good part of the day is spent prospecting and making sales presentations.

William (Bill) Baker, Principal and Founder,

William Baker & Associates, Inc. (Atlanta, GA), says it is very difficult to build a viable financial advisory practice on a commission basis because you cannot do the needed amount of business planning if you don't have recurring income. "If you're always having to hustle to get the next commission you're put in the position of being so focused on the next commission that you can lose concern for your current clients," he says. As a result, Bill transitioned his business from transactional to fee-based, which he feels allows him to serve his clients more thoroughly.

Bill suggests that the scandals within American industry, including the financial services sector, indicate a breakdown within our system. Ultimately, he says, it is the individual firm and advisor that you must rely upon. "Most advisors want to do the best job for their client, but if they are getting bad information and the checks-and-balances are taken out of the system, then their clients, inadvertently, may not get good advice."

One solution is for advisors to offer specific investment vehicles to their clients. Some only offer non-proprietary[1] products and outside research. Others will do an extensive analysis between what their firms offer and what is available outside of the firm. Such advisors have thoroughly studied all the available alternatives and are able to confidently present a good financial solution to their clients.

It is worth emphasizing that commissions are not inherently bad. Many times, as a few of our role models indicate, charging a commission is actually less expensive for their clients.

The Value of Expert Advice

Many people believe that they can or should make their own investment decisions by using either a local discount service or the Internet. Some people—those with extensive training in finances and the time to devote to the process—can make their own decisions, but most people are wise to incorporate the advice of financial professionals. Even those with the time and knowledge to invest on their own are well advised to get a second opinion from a qualified professional.

Thomas (Tom) B. Gau, CPA, CFP®, CRIA, Principal, Oregon Pacific Financial Advisors, Inc (Ashland, OR) says that when he conducts seminars he often highlights all of the errors that an investor can make on whatever topic he happens to be discussing. The point is, a small mistake on a small investment costs a small amount of money. However, a small mistake on a large investment costs a large sum of money.

[1] Some firms pay higher commissions if the advisor sells a proprietary (home-grown) product or service. Additionally, some firms put pressure on their salespeople to promote such products because of the increased profit margin for the firm. This practice is discouraged by industry regulators, yet it is still a common practice. Products, such as mutual funds, created by the firm, generate greater commissions than a similar mutual fund not owned by the brokerage firm. Note that it is not limited to mutual funds. Any non-exchange traded item, such as bonds, OTC stocks, unit investment trusts, and financial plans often have built-in additional profit for the firm and incentive for the representative.

He tells a humorous, but pertinent joke regarding paying for expertise. "Imagine," he says, "if an investor is jogging down the street and says, 'I have a pain in my chest. It's hurting me. I better see a doctor." The doctor says, "You'd better see a heart specialist." The investor goes to the cardiologist and discovers he needs a heart transplant. And the investor says, "Wow, thank you very much for the diagnosis. I'll find some heart transplant books on the Web and I'll do the operation myself."

By showing people all of the disastrous mistakes that can be made, Tom accomplishes three things:

1. He alerts them to numerous dangers that investors face because they are not highly educated in certain areas. Fore-warned is fore-armed.
2. He helps people avoid "small errors" that could destroy their futures. He asks the question, "When was the last time you retired? Are you willing to risk your 40 years worth of accumulation in your 401(k) plan by making one mistake and having the majority of your money go to the government? Are you willing to risk that?" (See the accompanying case study on page 15 for an example.)
3. He helps people realize that they are in the hands of a highly competent individual.

Tom says there are three questions that should be posed to every investor:

1. "When was the last time you did everything picture-perfect on a highly complicated matter the very first time you tried it?
2. "Are you willing to make one small mistake that messes up your entire final picture?" And the last question is,
3. "Is your financial advisor current on all the income tax laws that will affect your retirement distribution?"

Transitioning to a Higher Level of Professionalism

Many financial representatives transition from a sales-oriented business to concentrate on what they do best – providing high-level, comprehensive advice and service. They interview clients more thoroughly and offer strategies that allow clients to attain their financial goals instead of persuading those clients to buy or sell something. Just like doctors, lawyers, CPAs and other professions, such advisors are hired to provide expert counsel, not to sell products. They receive fees for their knowledge, specialized skills, and experience.

The chart on page 14 shows some of the key differences between the traditional financial representative and a high-level financial advisor.

Perhaps the best way to explain the difference between the old and new models of business is offered by Brian W. Puckett, JD, CPA/PFS, Brian Puckett Retirement Advisors, LLC (Oklahoma City, OK). "Being

OLD MODEL	NEW MODEL
Sales Representatives	Financial Advisors
Broker	Consultant
Commissions	Commissions and/or Fee
Trades Create Revenue	Knowledge Creates Revenue
Individual	Team
Stock Picking	Portfolio Allocation & Diversification
Unrelated Transactions	Comprehensive, Unified Solution
Hidden Costs	Transparency of Costs
Charge for Trades	Charge for Advice
Generalists	Specialists
Sales Culture	Service Culture

a financial advisor is a huge responsibility. It also feels wonderful to deliver peace of mind to a client. By becoming a steward of their wealth, I make sure that everything works the way it's supposed to, and I'm very clear about the fact that responsibilities have been delegated to my firm and me. Someone in that position has to be willing to step up to the plate and do things right."

According to Brian, "It is crucial for the average investor to recognize that their investment life is very, very important and they cannot completely get rid of the responsibility for making sure that it all turns out the way they want it to. But what they can do with a lot of this money management, tax planning, and wealthy management is to delegate it. Once they've found a good advisor that they can trust, they then can focus on the areas of their lives that they can't delegate, which are even more important than money to them. For example, they can't delegate the enrichment of their spiritual life. They can't delegate being a better spouse to their husband or wife. They can't delegate being a better father to their children."

Brian explains that once an investor has delegated the responsibility for wealth management to a trusted advisor, they can spend their time and talents doing many other important things with their lives. The following case study illustrates this concept.

The concept of stewardship permeates the thought processes of all of the advisors in this book—although they use different terms. They are able to make a big difference in the lives of the people they work with. They pride themselves on helping others and contributing to the welfare of individuals and society.

Making the Transition

Each advisor has interesting stories to tell about the challenges of developing a high-level advisory practice. Following are three examples.

A COSTLY ERROR

Thomas (Tom) Gau, Principal of Oregon Pacific Financial Advisors, Inc. tells this story:

"Late last year a prospective client met with me seeking advice on what to do with some problems he was having with his $1.4 million IRA. Here are the facts:

1. The prospect's mother passed away at the end of 1999 and had an IRA value of approximately $2.2 million. He was the sole beneficiary of this IRA.
2. The prospect rolled over the money from his mother's IRA into his during 2000.
3. The prospect also held other assets jointly with his mother and no one informed him -- neither the accountant nor his stock broker -- that his mother's estate might be subject to estate taxes.
4. The client received a significant income tax bill from the IRS for incorrectly filing his 2000 income tax return and not filing a federal estate tax return form 706.
5. The IRA had declined in value from $2.2 million to $1.4 million.

Unfortunately, there were a number of mistakes made on this transaction.

The total net worth of his mother as of the date of death was $3.6 million. This was a taxable estate since it exceeded the exemption amount in that year of $650,000. He was incorrectly informed that he did not need to add up all the assets of the estate since many of the assets were held in a variety of ways: the IRA with the beneficiary, his mom's real estate as joint tenants with him, and the rest of her assets in the name of her trust.

In addition to this, the IRA was subject to income taxation because only a spouse may roll over the money into his IRA. Obviously, since he was not a spouse, the entire $2.2 million was taxable all in one year!

Now, to add fuel to the fire, the portfolio was significantly invested in technology stocks in 1999 and these were hit hard by the bear market of 2000 to 2002. In fact, the value of his portfolio fell over 50 percent from its peak when he inherited it to its low at the end of 2002.

In addition to this, the prospect also engaged in a prohibited transaction by rolling over the IRA money into his IRA and, therefore, he was also subject to paying penalties on top of all these taxes.

The final result was that the total amount of taxes and penalties due to the government was over $2,000,000 on this inheritance. His IRA was not enough to pay off this liability and therefore the prospective client was forced not only to liquidate his entire IRA, but also had to sell his residence and almost all of his other assets to pay off this debt to the government.

To make matters even worse, he had to move to Florida to live with his parents until he could get his feet back on the ground financially. Unfortunately, his wife could not take this any longer and decided to divorce him as well!

It is important to note that the tax was due on the distribution of the value of the IRA at the time of the inheritance, and not at the date it was distributed to him a few years later.

The taxation on mom's IRA could have been deferred if he would have established an Inherited IRA!"

Example #1: Cella Quinn of Cella Quinn Investment Services had to fight her way into the financial services business in 1972. She applied for the job of financial representative at one of the largest brokerage firms in the United States, but says she was rejected because it was a male-dominated industry. Cella was finally able to obtain a position, but only if she would move from New York City, where none of the managers would hire her, to Omaha, NE.

Cella quickly saw the futility of trading stocks for clients and realized that the long-term approach to investing was most logical, despite the prevailing culture of her firm at that time. She began recommending mutual funds because the fund managers selected the unrecognized values in the same way Warren Buffet, one of the most famous investors of all time, did. (Her Warren Buffet story is told later in the book.) Cella and her clients find the compounding power of mutual funds really helps build wealth.

Example #2: Mark Little, Founder and Creator of The Freedom Experience®. (San Antonio, TX) had followed the mutual fund and stock market since age 12. His initial job with an investment firm was as a sales representative; however, he soon found he didn't like the traditional, transactional sales culture. After the October 1987 crash, he decided to open his own financial planning firm. Finding a brokerage firm willing to sponsor a 27-year-old was a daunting challenge. He talked to the

A TRUSTED ADVISOR

An elderly couple, described by Brian Puckett of Brian Puckett Retirement Advisors, LLC as "some of the smartest, neatest, genuine people I've ever met," first met him after years of investing with two or three of the largest brokerage firms in the world. Overall, they had about 20 different accounts, all sorts of different insurance policies and investments, and a sound estate plan. But they didn't really understand how everything fit together. They were spending a few hours every week going over their financial plan and discussing it.

Prior to meeting Puckett, they always felt that their various financial representatives regularly talked them into one "great" investment or another. They never really had a cohesive game plan customized to fulfill their goals and objectives.

Puckett created a strategic plan that provided a coordinated approach to attaining their life goals. These clients agreed that by engaging Puckett as their wealth steward, they were able to enjoy a greater quality of life.

When the husband passed away, Puckett was right there to help the widow rearrange accounts and make crucial decisions about her finances and estate.

Says Puckett, "She now spends a lot of her time working on volunteer projects with the church, with needy children, and spending time with friends. She feels the freedom to pursue and enjoy the things that really matter in her life."

founder of a firm in Connecticut, whom, according to Mark, "eventually stopped laughing and said that my telephone call to him was the most humorous and brazen call he had received in a long time, and finally added, 'I don't know why, but I'll give you a chance.'"

For the next few years he slowly built his practice until he realized that he wanted to bring his business to even higher levels of professionalism. In 1999, he made the extraordinarily difficult decision to work with only 17 of his then current clients and would only take on new client relationships that met certain stringent criteria. As of this writing, he now has 100 select clients to whom he provides exemplary service.

Example #3: George Jackson, President of Jackson Retirement Planning, Inc. never really had to make a transition because he started off as a CPA with a major CPA firm and grew up with the consulting mentality. Says George, "I take a consultative approach with my clients in the investment arena, give them options, and am not going to try to peddle something to them. Instead, I show them alternative A, and alternative B, and then explain the pros and cons between them."

It's All About You

The main reason these advisors transitioned their business was to offer their clients something even better.

Mike Piershale of Piershale Financial Group sums it all up when he talks about the benefits of transitioning from a commission-based sales representative to a fee-based financial planner. He believes it eliminates the potential conflict of interest when making investment recommendations and allows him to work at a much higher professional level. As a result, he believes that his firm now delivers much better client service.

The five key areas to financial success are: retirement (planning or income), insurance, investments, taxes, and estate planning.

In Conclusion

The advisors in this book have overcome some major obstacles to set up or get hired by businesses that keep all of a client's interests in mind. It means getting to know a client's "whole picture," setting up personalized plans, and keeping track of people and portfolios. High-level advisors find that steering away from a transaction-based business operation and being as open as possible with clients makes for a better working relationship. They like the satisfaction of serving clients without the pressure of pushing products.

◆◆◆

Levey on Integrity

"Integrity is probably the single most important component from which our clients, our peers, our friends and our family gauge their comfort with us. It serves as a catalyst for trust. The more people recognize the integrity within me, the more trust and comfort they'll have in me, my company, and my recommendations. In that regard, integrity, trust and my ability to be a valuable tool for my clients are permanently intertwined. Integrity is the key that unlocks the door, behind which lies all of the knowledge we, as planners, need to best serve those who place their trust in us.

The higher the level of trust a client has in me, the more they share with me. The more they share with me, the more I'm able to serve them. The more I'm able to serve them, the more significant the impact I can make in their lives. And, making a positive impact in the lives of those I serve and their families is why I'm in this business.

For these reasons, integrity is one of the single most important values I can have. Without it, I'm nothing. To that end, it serves as the fuel which powers the engine of my business."

Yale Levey, CFP®
Managing Director
Roseland Financial Group, LLC

Chapter 3

Who Are These Financial Advisors?

This chapter is dedicated to the spirit of caring that permeates everything these advisors do and defines who they are as individuals. This spirit becomes the driving force in almost all facets of their personal and work lives, including:

- Who they choose to work with and for
- The business model or approach they employ
- The associates that they work with and how they choose those associates
- How they position themselves with their clients
- The attitudes and capabilities of other professionals they work with
- What they go through to ensure that they continue to deliver excellent service
- How they approach a client relationship and what they do to maintain and enhance those relationships
- How they make a difference in the lives of the people they touch

Perhaps the best way of putting it is, the spirit of caring defines the "why" behind everything that they do. It often constitutes their personal and corporate missions in life and is incorporated into the integrity statement at the beginning of each chapter.

The following examples show the breadth and

depth of caring that these advisors evidence for all people that they touch; they are loosely divided into three main areas:

1. Helping clients and community
2. Office atmosphere
3. Enriching the financial services community

As you read the examples, keep in mind that such activities and attitudes should be part of your criteria when choosing an advisor. Of course, each person has his or her own unique needs, so some flexibility is needed. However, you should try to choose advisors whose philosophies on life are similar to yours. If you're concerned with leaving a legacy for your family, for example, look for an advisor who has similar aspirations and who has helped others accomplish similar goals.

Helping Clients and Community—In the first chapter you learned how Mike Piershale gave up his practice and became involved in a ministry to help needy children attend church and learn basic moral values. He made a huge difference in the lives of those youngsters during the years he devoted to them. Now, he continues to make a difference in the lives of all the people he touches by holding regular classes for friends, clients, church members and colleagues on a number of financial and self-improvement topics. Mike has extended his reach into countries such as India, Uruguay and Romania by teaching financial topics to church leaders while participating in missions trips. He is a person who believes in empowering people to become more knowledgeable than they already are.

The ability to provide high levels of service often depends on the firm the advisor is associated with. If a client is merely "another account" to a firm, chances are that firm-centered view prevents a representative or advisor from going the extra mile to create a truly client-centric business. This means a client is likely getting short-changed.

Prior to their current affiliations, the advisors in this book had to choose a firm that allowed them to truly provide the level of service and advice they wanted to offer their clients. In some cases they became "independent" of the large firms or switched affiliations.

Good examples are Craig Pluta, Co-founder of ReAct! Group and First VP of Ziegler Investment Services Group (Milwaukee, WI), and his partner Chris Doughty who made the decision that rather than being jacks-of-all-trades, to "know and understand everything they could about the retirement market and the planning process." Based on surveys of what clients and firms wanted, they developed a process called the Retirement Action Plan (ReAct!), which provided a high level of service to their clients. At that time, they were working under the umbrella of a large broker-dealer that frowned on advisors providing services beyond the "norm" for the corporation. Simultaneously, Craig and Chris felt uncomfortable about the pressure they were under to promote the firm's proprietary products.

When searching for another firm, they received numerous offers of "up-front money[1]" from most of the larger firms in their area. But they soon realized that most of the large firms are virtual mirror images of each other, and by merely taking the best monetary offer, they would be compromising their dream. However, that didn't happen when they sat down with the executive running Ziegler Investment Services Group (their current affiliation). He said, "I'm going to offer you something that is far more valuable than money. I'm going to offer you a home where you can pursue everything that I know you're trying to do, and I will clear the road blocks for you so you can make it happen. And, that is going to be worth much more than somebody writing you a check up front." Craig and Chris looked at him and said, "You're talking our language." They sat down, ironed out the details, and Ziegler has been the firm they have been affiliated with ever since.

Being active in the community and using one's talents to help others is another demonstration of caring. This can take many forms, from being involved with scouting, to developing community centers, to being a Big Brother or Big Sister. Mark Little, founder of The Freedom Experience®, goes that

[1] Up-front money refers to an industry practice where excellent good financial representatives or advisors are offered cash bonuses if they switch to another firm. The firm pays the rep/advisor to switch and then, hopefully, recaptures the money from the increased commissions it receives from the clients that follow the rep/advisor to the new firm.

LENDING A HELPING HAND

Mark Little's office (The Freedom Experience®) has adopted a United Way agency called Respite Care of San Antonio. When his firm conducts its regular "Focus on the Future" meetings for its entire community of clients, Mark talks about personal and family values and includes a discussion on Respite Care. Respite Care deals with mentally and physically challenged youth many of whom are in crisis. Often they are victims of either abuse or neglect; many are disabled kids who have been abused or neglected. About one-third of them are babies. The head of Respite gives an update at the meeting and also gives each client opportunities to help the children.

Prior to the Focus on the Future forum, Respite Care provides a wish list of items they need, and Mark's team forwards that list to its clients.

The Freedom Experience's clients then bring baby food or diapers or provide other types of help.

Some of Mark's retired clients have even donated their time to hold and rock a baby with Downs Syndrome. This is a major help to the agency because it doesn't have the staff to do such things.

As Mark says, "We just create opportunities for our clients to get involved. We don't push it; it's an awareness thing."

In a "Quality of Life Enhancer" exercise, some clients find that they are searching for opportunities to make a difference in the community – something that is also highly satisfying. Mark helps find ways for them to help.

extra step by helping his philanthropically-oriented clients get actively involved in special causes.

Office Atmosphere—Although team development is discussed in a subsequent chapter, it's important to point out here that how an advisor treats his or her staff is a good indication of how the advisor and team work with clients. It is common knowledge that employees who are satisfied and feel valued by their companies are more productive (better) employees and more responsive to the company's clients. Office atmosphere sets the framework for excellent customer service.

In the previous chapter we learned how Cella Quinn pursued a career in financial services when odds were against her. While that drive and determination continues to serve her, it only partly reflects the concern she has for the people who surround her. She lovingly admits that her employees and clients are her family. In fact, Cella has funded special insurance policies for employees that go far beyond key-man insurance. Provisions have been made for them to eventually inherit the business, along with the money to run it. This will enable them to take care of her clients. It also enables them to take care of themselves and to have enough money to take care of their children and grandchildren.

Michael Searcy, of Searcy Financial Services, Inc, creates a real family atmosphere in the office. This office environment is strongly tied to Mike's personal philosophy on life. He says that when he was 23-years-old, he developed a personal philosophy of life by developing a priority system that he still follows to this day, and intends to follow for the rest of his life. "I believe that if I keep my priorities in proper order – 1, God; 2, family; 3, clients and friends; and 4, myself – my journey through life will be stable and prosperous. I am convinced that if I take care of priorities No. 1 through No. 3 in their proper order, then my needs, goals and dreams will surely be met," he says.

Mike has a great office atmosphere. All his staff members work closely as a coordinated team. They, of course, have birthday parties for each staff member, holiday parties, and many other typical gatherings that you would see in a close knit group. It's the following underlying philosophy of family and clients first that truly differentiates Mike's office and is best illustrated by three brief examples:

1. When Mike hired a young man to join the staff he said, "I want you to understand something. When your child has things that need care, or if he's got a baseball game or a recital or something at school, and you're not there to participate in his life, I'm going to fire you." The new employee looked at Mike oddly. Mike explained, "We're in the planning business. The operative word is planning. You can still get your work done and be at your son's event."

2. An employee had a new baby and was encouraged to bring the baby to the office. Mike recalls one time when he was walking around, holding the baby, talking on the phone.
3. He regularly introduces his clients to his grandchildren whenever they happen to be at the office.

Enriching the Financial Services Community—High-level advisors continually learn from one another and from other experts in the financial services profession. The mark of a true professional is the acknowledgement that there is always more to learn, a better way of doing things, new approaches to take, and different strategies that can be employed.

The most common method to gain this information is to attend industry conferences and workshops and do a tremendous amount of studying and research. At the conferences and workshops, financial professionals listen to knowledgeable speakers who offer high-quality information based on extensive experience. Tom Gau of Oregon Pacific Financial Advisors is one of the most recognized industry speakers in the nation and a coach/mentor to more than 100,000 financial professionals.

Tom spends a portion of each week helping other advisors become more successful. He and his coaching partner, Ken Unger teach others how to be more successful in the financial services business by emulating the business practices and financial planning strategies employed by Tom in his day-to-day activities.

Generally, business people are hesitant to help their potential competition by giving away trade secrets. Tom and Ken feel that the only way their industry can advance is to assist like-minded, high-level professionals in becoming even better than they already are.

How This All Translates

It is easy to see how the philosophies of these advisors affect how they view themselves as part of an integrated team; that team is comprised of you—the client, the advisor and advisory staff, and strategic alliances with other professionals.

All take their jobs very seriously and do everything in their power to fulfill their primary duties of helping people identify, define, and achieve their personal and financial goals.

In Conclusion

A tremendous spirit of caring is revealed in all of these advisors. Without this attention and consideration of others' needs, an advisor cannot do an adequate job of helping people fulfill their personal and financial goals.

Each demonstrates the philosophy in different ways, but the net result is the delivery of an extraordinary level of professionalism to their clients.

◆◆◆

The Trust Equation

Prepare

Research & Review

Objectives

Communication

Evaluate & Execute

Systems

Synchronize & Synergy

Chapter 4

The Importance of PROCESS

One of the major distinctions between high-level financial advisors and financial representatives is their strict adherence to specific disciplines and processes. In other words, they follow systematic, proven methods to chart the correct financial course for each client.

When you take a car trip, there are usually a number of roads that will allow you to reach your destination. However, some routes are more direct and efficient than others. Similarly, in choosing a financial destination, some routes are more direct and provide more consistent results, while others are fraught with danger or delays. If you have an important goal to attain, such as your financial future, why take a chance on getting random results – perhaps missing your goal completely? Instead, you can significantly boost your probability of financial success by working with an advisor who has a proven track record of helping others reach similar goals.

Each of the high-level advisors interviewed for this book learned through experience and education numerous investment disciplines and methodologies that have proven effective over the years. These strategies are the same ones used by sophisticated money managers and investors throughout the world.

Using Qualified Professionals to Achieve Superior Results

Consider this analogy: If you or a loved one needed a complex surgery, you would seek out a surgeon with a high level of training, a successful history of performing similar operations, and substantial knowledge of the most recent medical advances. You would ask other professionals for referrals, check on the surgeon's reputation, and simultaneously learn all you could about the medical condition.

You would also expect the surgeon and his or her entire staff to systematically follow an established process or procedure. This process would probably start with a thorough examination, taking into account your overall physical condition. Next, your condition and surgery would be explained to you and all your questions answered. If you agree to the operation, additional examinations may occur. On the day of the operation, surgery team members would be present to perform their various functions. After the procedure, you would be checked and monitored. Then, by following the doctor's recommended regimen for recovery, and with periodic checkups, you would find yourself in good health again.

The same holds true for all the important financial advisors in your life. These advisors might include an accountant, attorney, trust specialists, and others. It's important to surround yourself with the best team you can draw upon—professionals who will help you maintain your maximum financial health.

You want to work with a high-level financial advisor with experience and a proven discipline, and one who has continually upgraded his or her knowledge. The advisor should have an excellent reputation, proven by ongoing records of success and high levels of service. This person should work with well-trained and highly educated associates, whose expertise also can be drawn upon.

In the surgery analogy, you will remember that responsibilities were shared by the patient and all the medical team members. The same is true in the financial world. You, the investor, must carry certain responsibilities, such as asking for and checking references, and then asking relevant questions of both the advisors and their references (the subject of chapter 7). In addition, you must understand the process, go for periodic follow-up evaluations, and, of course, keep in contact with the advisor.

A Dual Responsibility

This book discusses your responsibilities as an investor, those of the advisor, and methods used to evaluate the performance of the advisor, your portfolio, and your relationship. At the same time, you are also being evaluated. That is because throughout the process, your advisors should constantly assess all components of your financial plan, including you. Advisors want their clients to communicate with them and to provide them with any changes or updates concerning their financial condition or objectives. This information may lead to some changes in your financial plan and/or portfolio. If you, or any other client, insist on a course of action that is contrary to your, or any other client's best interests, and against the advisor's business philosophy, the adviser may decline to work with you (or any other client) in the future. Other things they consider:

- Are your investment and service expectations reasonable?
- Are you willing/able to follow advice?
- Are you teachable?
- Do you share the same investment philosophy?
- Are your needs/goals something that they (the advisors) can help you fulfill? (That is, is it within their area of expertise?)

The next 10 chapters discuss a process that allows you to select, monitor, and evaluate your advisors. You'll learn what an advisor does for you and receive an excellent overview into the practices of high-level financial advisors and their teams.

It is important to realize that a lot of the activities within this process overlap, depend on each other, or occur simultaneously. The process is similar to the movements of gears within a watch. If one part of the mechanism breaks down, the watch does not fulfill its function of keeping accurate time.

Importance of Process

Each advisor interviewed for this book was asked to rate the importance of having a process for preparing investment recommendations. All said that it was exceedingly important or vital. A process helps ensure consistent results. It makes sure that nothing slips between the cracks. It helps ensure ongoing excellence. It eliminates much randomness from the equation. And, most importantly, the process is constantly being refined or improved upon.

A process is a systematic procedure for accomplishing a goal. Each of the advisors has specific processes for things such as:

- Choosing and monitoring investments
- Keeping track of important client documents
- Scheduling ongoing contact with clients
- Creation of newsletters
- Ensuring client satisfaction

A good example is George Jackson of Jackson Retirement Planning, Inc. who says they systematize everything. "Everything we do has a Standard Operating Procedure (SOP). From the moment a client walks in for the first time, or a client calls, or someone expresses interest in our service, we have a SOP we go through on how they are invited to the office and what we do when we first meet them. If they become a client, they will continue to get a series of procedures and processes so that we give them exemplary service. The key to great customer service, I believe, is consistency. People want consistency in their experience with us. So we focus on giving clients a consistent experience. We systematize everything."

Exemplary service and advice don't happen by accident. It is the result of years of study and refinement.

One of the characteristics of star performers in any industry or profession is their ability to constantly find ways to improve. After all, one-hundredth of a second can represent the difference between first and second place in certain sports. Knowing just a little more can be the difference between being an expert and a noted authority.

Chris Doughty of ReAct! Group, says that his group's study of the best practices in the industry has become a process in and of itself. Their studies have led them to develop numerous processes to cover every aspect of their retirement planning business.

According to Chris, "The reason having a process is so critical is because if a process isn't in place, an advisor will do things differently each time. There is no consistency in any of the approaches being used, and I just don't understand how someone can run a business that way."

Eric Hutchinson of Hutchinson/Ifrah Financial Services, Inc. explains their system called The Retirement Discovery Process™. "It is a structured process to make sure that we do the right things, ask the right questions, look at the right documents, and so on."

He explains to potential clients that he and his team have a comprehensive process to help people like themselves deal with retirement issues. When he explains the process, it brings a measure of relief to potential clients who are then more confident they have come to the right place. They realize that these people know what they are doing. Eric says the key is having a defined process. "It helps to have it labeled and graphic, so you can see the various steps and stages. It helps potential clients get the message that they are not the only people dealing with those issues, and that other people have dealt with these same issues successfully. You can immediately see a change in their body language. They relax."

The Hutchinson/Ifrah process has numerous components. It begins with an extensive analysis of a client's goals, vision and values, which are articulated in writing. The educational segment teaches basic concepts of successful investing and incorporates modern portfolio theory, how money is managed, risk, etc. Everything is put in writing with The Retirement Discovery Guide Map™, which becomes both a roadmap and a reference during future meetings. Regular reviews and meetings allow them to make appropriate adaptations to the plan based upon changing circumstances within the family, such as a new grandchild, or changes in the economy.

An added benefit of having defined processes that are followed by all members of the team is that if something happens to the primary advisor, the client will continue to receive the same level of service from other team members. Says Eric, "They realize that they're going to get similar service from any of the planners on our team. It also provides comfort when they see the depth of our organization. We have a very structured way of doing things." Eric says that if something might happen to him or any one of the firm's planners, there is a whole organization that is doing the same kind of thing, so they could take the ball and run with it. He points out that there are many solo practitioners in the industry who may be very successful, but if something happens to them, what will their clients do?

Bill Baker of William Baker & Associates, Inc. created the following graph to show some of the key components of his company's processes. He emphasizes that the client or prospect has to be given priority over the process. In other words, an initial part of the process is getting acquainted with a person to see if he or she will be a match for the company's services. "We'll adjust the process depending on the depth of service that the client requires. For instance, if they already have done estate planning and specifically want our investment management services, that would be an adjustment to our process and deliverables."

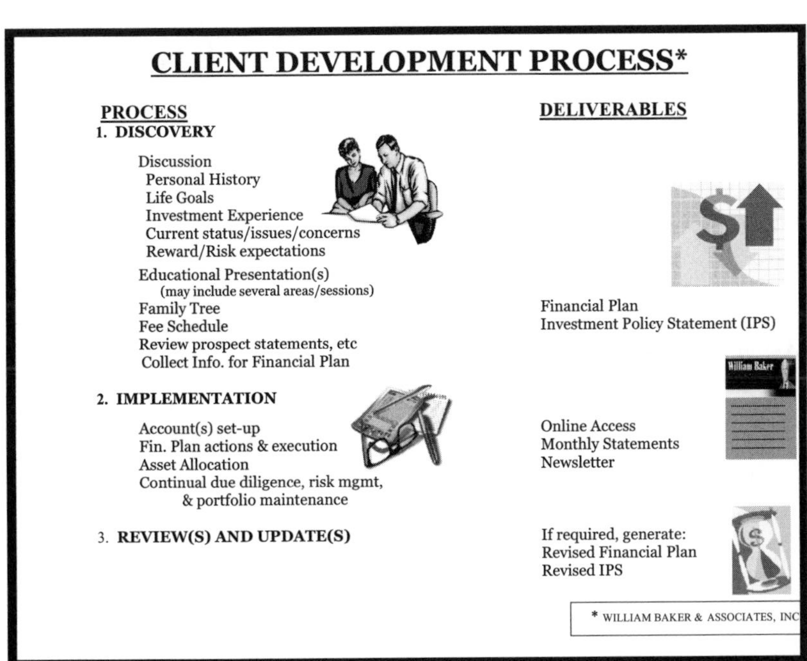

Unfortunately, many representatives focus on individual products and services offered by their firms and often fail to identify the many ways an investment solution can be crafted. As a result, clients only get part of a solution. Like the watch, all the pieces may be there, but it takes a skilled watchmaker to put them together into a working timepiece. High-level advisors are like master watchmakers who can redesign the watch. If advisors have a defined, proven process, that leaves very little, if anything, to chance.

Procedures to Help You Succeed

The acronym PROCESS is the basis for the next seven major topics within the book. You'll be taken through the basics of a process for finding, meeting, evaluating, working with, and monitoring advisors. At the same time, you'll see aspects of each of these seven concepts from the advisor's perspective.

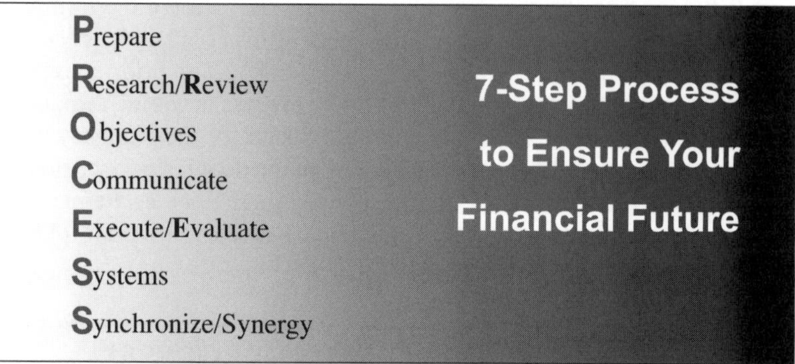

The next two chapters explain how both you and the advisor must *prepare* (the first step in process) for a financial meeting. As an investor, you must get referrals, define your objectives, and perform due diligence. Advisors prepare by increasing their knowledge and by creating strategic alliances with other professionals. While they are reviewing your objectives with you, discussing reasonable expectations, and deciding if you are a "correct fit" for their style of doing business, you should evaluate them and decide if you feel comfortable with them and their business approach. Again, it's like a watch: Many things are happening simultaneously.

So, what constitutes expert financial advice? Here are some of the factors a financial advisor should consider when working with a client:

1. Determine precisely what a client's desired outcomes or objectives are.
2. Evaluate all of a client's finances—insurance policies, real estate holdings, financial investments and private holdings, estate plans—in light of the client's objectives and the big picture.

3. Consider the tax and legal consequences of each individual item or group of items held by the individual or within different legal entities or structures. Alternative approaches should also be considered.
4. Include appropriate technologies.
5. "Know what they don't know," and be willing to bring in additional outside expert advice to assist in attaining client objectives. That is, use a team approach when appropriate.
6. Orchestrate all the experts' knowledge and efforts to produce the best results.
7. Develop precise, written plans to accomplish macro and tactical goals.
8. Develop contingency plans.
9. Master approaches to help guard against changing market conditions.
10. Adapt plans when necessary.
11. Ensure that goals will be accomplished, even without the advisor's direct help.
12. Make sure a client understands the essence of the plans.

Michael Searcy of Searcy Financial Services, Inc. emphasizes that having a well-thought-out process also allows for customization based upon his client's particular needs. Neither he, nor any of the other advisors, will let procedures get in the way of the relationship. Mike says, "My relationship with my client is more important than any process I employ to accumulate and preserve wealth. This relationship grows out of an analysis of the client's continually changing goals, in-depth discussions throughout the year, a clear framework of their expectations for the future, and cooperation with the client's all-important comfort zone related to risk-taking in the investment marketplace."

If advisors can't articulate their process, then there probably isn't a process. This means they're not the type of advisor you would want to work with.

In Conclusion

Each investor has an obligation to find out whether his or her advisor is sales or process driven. When you interview an advisor, he or she should be able to explain his or her process to you in detail, and, even better, be able to put it in writing.

◆◆◆

Little on Integrity

"We help people make smart choices about their money so they can accomplish their goals for the reasons that are most important to them in life. To create a relationship supporting that vision, trust is required. I have to trust that the client is sincerely conveying everything to us that we will need to know to help each of them create the greatest probability that their financial plans and goals unfold properly.

Our wealth management firm serves the role of Personal Chief Financial Officer for our small community of clients. The responsibility is great and confidence is required by both parties to make the relationship work well. While trust is something that is earned over time, it has to be given up-front before any client has the self-assurance to place the money in an advisor's hands.

We have implemented a process which allows a client to do the proper due diligence in a reasonably short period of time. At the end of our initial client meeting, if the relationship is going to work, we both know it. If there's a fit, and trust has been established on both sides, then we move forward. If it's not a good fit, it's obvious to everyone and we politely disengage.

I believe people are either ethical or they're not. Period! I feel the best guiding principle, regardless of faith, is the golden rule. Do unto others what you would have them do unto you simply means asking yourself, in every situation confronting you in life, how would I like to be treated if the roles were reversed? This is a simple and elegant philosophy that has served my firm well for the nearly 20 years of our existence."

Mark Little, Founder/Creator
The Freedom Experience®

Chapter 5

PREPARE: Finding a Competent and Trustworthy Advisor

PROCESS: Prepare

- To make ready, fit, or qualified.
- To provide with what is needed; outfit.
- To make preparations; get ready.

"It's important for prospective clients to do everything they can to identify a competent financial advisor. To me, that is more important than anything," says Brian Puckett of Brian Puckett Retirement Advisors. "In other words, it's not what investment you pick. It's not what tax strategy to use. It really boils down to identifying a competent, ethical financial advisor because if they are honest and ethical and know what they are doing, they're going to take care of you even if there are things that you [the client] don't know about financial planning."

Brian adds a very important point, "Unfortunately, such advisors are a lot rarer than most investors realize."

What If?

The hypothetical story that follows was created to help you understand what you need to know to find a competent advisor. Although fictitious, this scenario sets the stage for much of this book.

John and Jane inherit $25 million from a great aunt, and go from rags to riches. After paying off a small amount of debt and meeting relatives they never knew existed, they want to invest their money wisely. They are well aware that most people who come into sudden wealth lose it very quickly. (Just consider the statistics of what happens to lottery winners. It is reported that 80 percent file for bankruptcy within five years of receiving their "big win.") John and Jane want to avoid making the same mistakes others have made. They don't have any wealthy friends to get advice from and realize that the phone calls they've received from every Tom, Dick, and Harry offering advice and service can't all be legitimate. And even if they were legit, how do they decide which "professional" is the right one for them?

They seek advice from their local banker who offers everything from CDs to mutual funds. Their accountant suggests municipal bonds and some tax approaches. They then visit local branches of three brokerage firms and larger banks only to discover that every one of the financial representatives they meet is a "personal wealth manager" who can put them in contact with the right team of people who "do this wealth management stuff all of the time." What a dilemma. What should this couple do? How do they find the right advisor? What skills, knowledge and experience should the advisor have? What investment approach should they take? What are the best solutions to their problems?

In reality, these same issues are faced by many investors, regardless of the amount of money involved or their sophistication level. While there are no absolute answers, it can pay to follow the advice and guidelines provided within this book. The advice comes from financial services experts, advisors, the government, and industry credentialing organizations. Topics include:

- Establishing financial goals
- Finding the right advisor(s)
- Getting referrals and checking references
- Questions advisors should ask you, and vice-versa
- Checking credentials

Developing Trust

Ultimately, you should choose an advisor based upon the trust equation, which is determined, in part, by your personal comfort level with them. Many of the advisors in this book agree that your comfort level is the final determining factor. Your comfort level, however, should be based upon a selection process that you go through. Your confidence in an advisor will increase (or decrease) as you learn about the experiences of other clients in situations similar to your own. By understanding the processes that should be in place and knowing about industry best practices and standards, you will be able to reasonably determine whether to employ a particular person, team, or organization to help you attain your long-term objectives.

Most of the advisors in this book agree that many investors do not know what to look for in an advisor. Too often investors are "babes in the woods" and have no way to evaluate an advisor's value, competence, or suitability. Such investors can easily fall prey to financial predators or become involved with financial incompetents. Fortunately, you and other investors can follow several guidelines to increase the probability of finding the right advisor.

It requires work on your part, or what is called "due diligence." It may seem burdensome, but remember everything that is at stake:

The following tips will help you find the right advisor and allow you to feel more confident about your financial decisions.

Learn About the Industry

You should take the time and responsibility to understand the basics of the capital markets. While explained more completely in Chapter 13, it is important to realize that high returns usually are associated with high risks; yet, substandard salespeople actively promote high returns. Depending upon your financial situation, it may be unwarranted to assume any more risk than absolutely necessary.

Yale Levey of Roseland Financial Group suggests that people do preliminary reading, go to workshops, or learn about the financial markets in any way possible. He finds it very helpful when people can tell him where they are financially and where they want to be.

The worst thing you can do is be completely blind to what happens in this industry and what motivates the people within it, such as how most financial sales representatives get paid.

It is also important that you do not fall under the illusion that you can blindly trust any company or institution. Financial firms spend hundreds of millions of dollars each year on advertising and sales promotions – trying to get you to personally identify with *the company* and trust *the company* and all of its advisors. Don't fall for it. You will be dealing with an individual representative or advisor, not the institution. A poor representative in a good company is obviously not a good choice.

The question is often raised, "But can't I just have someone direct me to a good advisor?" Essentially this person is saying, "Can't I just delegate the task?" Not really.

Brian Puckett says, "I advise perspective clients to take the hiring of a financial advisor very seriously and to really exercise the same amount of due diligence in making that decision as any other important decision that they make. The selection of an advisor is one of those decisions that the client can't delegate. All other decisions for the management of their assets can be delegated to the advisors and money managers, but the selection of the advisor or advisory team is the one decision that they have to make on their own. Just as I, or any other competent advisor have a well-thought-out and systematized method of determining what investments to select for a client, so too should the client have a process to help them select the appropriate advisor. And it shouldn't be just because your friend at the country club uses the advisor. It shouldn't be, 'Hey, I'll use this advisor because I like him or her.' I think that it should be based on trust, and that trust should be granted only to an advisor who has the ability to give the client's family lasting financial security and to be the steward of their family's wealth, not only for their own generation, but for generations to come."

Choosing an Advisor Takes Time

One of the biggest mistakes people make is they don't dedicate enough time and effort to finding and selecting the appropriate advisor even when they accept the responsibility.

Brian says that many times certain investors seem reluctant to spend time searching for the "right" advisor. However, no matter how much time it takes, you need to do your homework when it comes to this particular task. The advisor you choose will set the stage for your economic future. Therefore, it is vital to choose wisely.

Learn About Yourself

Before you begin your search, there is one extraordinarily important preliminary task that you must do. Failure to do this is a virtual guarantee that you will not find the ideal advisor. You must carefully think about what you want your money to do for you and your family, and you must decide what you want from an advisor. Granted, the vast majority of people don't know what they want in an advisor until they've worked with one or more of the financial sales representatives out there. Even then, it's difficult for people to know what they want because the sales-dominated, product/service-oriented suggestions represent the only experience these investors have had with financial advisors.

Therefore, prior to meeting with an advisor, Yale Levey suggests staying focused on what's most important to you regarding both financial and non-financial issues. "Write down each point ahead of time. If investors can articulate what is meaningful to them then, whether consciously or unconsciously, they'll be looking to see if the advisor broaches those issues, and that will help clarify whether there is a match between the advisor and themselves."

For example, if you want to preserve your wealth for retirement and for estate purposes, you'll want an advisor who would act in an appropriately conservative manner. You would expect such a person to advise against risky investments. Craig Pluta of the ReAct! Group concurs, saying, "Part of being an advisor is being the advocate of the client. It means not always taking the easy path of just going along with what they may initially want but, instead, being ready to disagree with the client or go against a course of action, saying 'It's not a good idea. I don't think you want to do that and here is why....,' when appropriate. Clients crave this kind of honesty."

In addition, you'd be wise to demand that the advisor have:

- An investment philosophy and process that matches your objectives
- A successful track record when working with people who have similar needs
- A good number of clients who have similar objectives (you don't want to be the only one – or one of very few –trying to conservatively preserve wealth)

You'd also expect the advisor to ask you a lot of penetrating questions in order to ensure a complete understanding of your needs – financial and non-financial. In many cases, their astute and penetrating questions will help you crystallize your goal even further. (Questions that you can ask yourself and that advisors may ask you are offered in the next chapter.)

It is only when the advisor has a thorough understanding of your needs, goals, desires, motivations, etc. – that is, really understands you as a person – than the appropriate financial plan or investment strategy can be crafted.

Evaluate Multiple Advisors

After you've learned about the industry and decided the essential services and the general type of advisor you want, you should interview several advisors before making your final selection. By that time, you will have refined and added criteria based upon the various interviews. The introductory meeting is usually free, and you get a chance to meet face-to-face, evaluate the advisor based on his or her questions, and judge how your questions are answered.

All of the advisors interviewed think that clients should meet with several advisors before making a decision. They know that they stand head-and-shoulders above their competition, and that if the client finds a better "personality fit" then they should work with that person. The only way to make that determination, however, is by meeting with multiple candidates.

To save time and to guarantee a consistent evaluation, create a series of questions that you want answered or an agenda that you wish to follow. You'll find topics of discussion and questions to ask potential advisors included in almost every chapter of this book.

Craig Pluta says that his team often tells prospects that it's fine if they interview a lot of different advisors because that's how they'll discover the biggest difference between how they and another advisor do business.

"They'll be able to see what we really do. We feel that the more people they see, the better we look. Other advisors help differentiate us. We find that people are somewhat surprised by, but appreciate, that piece of advice."

Craig and his partner, Chris Doughty, use a process that includes asking people a lot of specific investment and goal-related questions. They also get to know them as people—essentially finding out what areas are of real concern to them. They'll talk about estate planning, educational funding, retirement planning, etc. to discover the areas of need and interest. Craig says, "It does no good to try to dazzle people with our knowledge in areas that are of no concern to them. What is important is to find out what concerns the client has and then concentrate on those issues."

Craig makes an important point: "It's about solving their problems, not us solving our problems. We don't say to someone, 'If an advisor doesn't ask you this question then it's a bad sign.'"

They don't have to. Clients often say, "Gee, no one else asked me that before." Craig and Chris just nod.

Chris says he believes that people are intuitively brilliant. People have great intuition and know when they are being dealt with honestly and ethically. "They should trust that intuition," he says.

Mark Little of The Freedom Experience® says, "I think people have a pretty good sense of smell. If an advisor is talking about golf and fishing, and not focusing on the important things, then people will pick that up."

Mark describes a situation during which he was interviewing an advisor who was applying for a job with his firm. This applicant was currently employed by a prestigious firm in New York City that was quite a bit larger than Mark's. The story is enlightening and offers numerous key points for selecting an advisor and firm.

Mark says: "So I asked him questions like 'what does your firm do to justify the 1 percent fee that you charge on each million dollars that you manage? That is, if I hand you $1 million, and am willing pay you $10,000 a year to manage it, what are you going to give me for that $10,000?' He didn't understand what I meant by that." So Mark took a different approach and asked how often he, as a client, would receive a call from the advisor if his portfolio were doing well. It turns out that this "prestigious" company hadn't made a proactive service call to two-thirds of its clients in more than a year.

Mark provides a list of his services, called the "10 Client Deliverables," to each of his clients. This is part of what he calls "The Freedom Experience®." (See page 40.)

A tremendous number of things can happen in a year. That's why it is so important for you to meet with your advisor on a regular basis. All of the advisors in this book meet with each of their clients at least once a year; often they have quarterly or semi-annual meetings with many of their clients. Life changes such as a new child, a death in the family, a divorce, a job change, or an inheritance can impact your financial and personal life, so it is incumbent on any high-level advisor to keep in touch with you.

Ask Peers for Referrals

When it comes to matters of wealth, you want to get referrals from people who are in a financial position similar to yours or from people who are knowledgeable about financial services professionals.

Further, Chris Doughty suggests that a person consult someone at their workplace who already has done all of the due diligence. For example, he knew of someone who had visited with nine different advisors and was willing to pass along the information that he had learned to friends and associates.

Ask Professionals for Referrals

An estate or trust attorney usually has a network of other professionals to draw upon. You probably wouldn't ask a criminal lawyer for the name of a good insurance agent or a wealth management team because they are not within their circle of influence. Therefore, only ask someone "in the know." Ask your accountant or attorney if he or she is associated with a particular advisor or if he or she could recommend one. Also make sure that you ask him or her for the name of an advisor who is a specialist in your particular situation.

Other Potential Sources of Referrals

In addition to asking reliable sources for referrals, consider contacting the financial editors of newspapers or magazines dealing with issues similar to yours—a pension magazine, for example. Other referral sources include the local chamber of commerce, your state's bar association, successful business owners in your area, and various industry associations, many of which have local chapters. A few phone calls can lead you to some excellent referrals.

Remember to interview multiple advisors. Visit the wealth specialists at banks and brokerage firms to evaluate their services; and as part of your interview, ask them who their competitors are—then visit them. Don't sign on the dotted line with anyone until you've done your homework. You have a lot at stake, just like John and Jane.

Additional Thoughts

Consider looking for an advisor who already has a successful practice. Mike Piershale offers an interesting analogy. He asks clients if they have ever gone out of town and tried to find a good restaurant. "If you drive

Ten Client Deliverables

Here is a summary of the 10 client deliverables that Mark Little and his firm, The Freedom Experience®, provide to their clients. Each investor should ask their advisor what their deliverables are.

1. Financial Road-map™: A complete and thorough annual update of your Financial Road-map™, with the focus on client, his/her values and goals, and benchmarking of progress. This deliverable includes an updated "Golden Years Projection," including written plans for cash reserves, each individual financial asset and goal, the estate, and all insurances.

2. Implementation Plan: Annual summary of the financial plan providing a simple chronological list of action steps required to create the greatest probability that you will stay on track with your financial plan over the years.

3. Quarterly Progress Reports: Simple summaries of your assets designed to show you the progress you are making against your benchmarked goals.

4. Asset Structure & Strategy Reviews: the goal of these semiannual discussions is to provide the "big picture" about your financial situation, give you a summary of the strategy going forward, and later review your implementation plan.

5. Income Tax Planning: Conduct a serious income tax plan with two objectives: To seek ways to reduce taxes and to make sure that there are no surprises in April.

6. Income Tax Preparation: During the first quarter of each year the firm will prepare your income tax return for you.

7. Estate: Once every five years, the firm will review and update your estate planning. The two objectives are, one, to establish a plan for your money to make it into the next generation and beyond and, two, create a structure that will bring your heirs closer together, avoiding conflicts about the money after your demise.

8. Goals: Proactively contact you prior to every "goal day" you have established to give you the game plan for the accomplishment of each of your goals.

9. Cash and Debt Management: Help you establish adequate cash reserves to handle financial issues that come up in life. This involves establishing a debt elimination plan as well as assistance with major purchases.

10. Insurance Review: Review every kind of insurance, recommend the right types and amounts of insurance, and ensure there are no coverage gaps, all of which might endanger the financial plan. They also will see what, if anything, can be done to reduce premiums.

up to a restaurant and there are no cars in the parking lot at lunchtime, you'd be well-advised to drive on. However, if the lot is packed with automobiles there is a better chance the food is going to be pretty good. Conceptually, there's not a lot of difference between that situation and our field. If you learn about one who is busy all the time, that alone can be a good indicator that the advisor knows what he or she is doing, especially if he or she has been around a long time. There's no way anyone can do this over a long period of time without knowing what he or she is doing, and gaining the confidence of the clients."

Mike also suggests new clients find a financial advisor who is successful within his or her own peer group or company. If the client can find an advisor who has been out there for several years and who is in the top five to ten percent of his or her company, that alone should give clients a strong indication that the advisor is very competent. "Good people eventually rise to the top," he says

Questions to Ask

The Certified Financial Planner Board of Standards, (CFP board) puts out a helpful brochure entitled "10 questions to ask when choosing a financial planner" (or almost any type of financial advisor). The brochure includes an interview checklist. These questions will help you interview and evaluate several financial planners to find the appropriate one for you.

1. What experience do you have? How long have you been in business? What types of people or companies do you work with? Describe your work experience relative to your current services.
2. What are your qualifications? What qualifies you to offer financial advice and what professional designations do you hold? Do you keep current with industry changes? How? Verify that any designations held are current.
3. What services do you offer? (Services depend on a number of factors including credentials, licenses, and areas of expertise. For example, advisors who sell insurance or securities products must have a different license for each.) What services *don't* you offer?
4. What is your approach to financial advice? What types of clients do you like to work with? Are you a generalist or specialist? (Make sure the advisor's viewpoint on investing is not too cautious or overly aggressive for you.) Will you carry out the financial recommendations developed for me or refer me to others who will do so?
5. Will you be the only person working with me? (If the advisor uses the services of other professionals, such as attorneys, tax specialists, insurance agents, get a list of their names to check on their backgrounds.) Will I be working directly with a client-relationship manager? If so, who is it? When will I meet him or her?

6. How will I pay for services? Note: Advisors can be paid in several ways:
   a) Salary. Who pays their salary?
   b) Fees charged on an hourly rate or a flat, one-time fee, which may be based on your level of wealth or the difficulty of the project.
   c) Commissions paid by you or others.
   d) Combination of fees and commissions.
   e) Fee-based advisors charge a percentage of assets under management only.
7. How much do you typically charge? (Get an estimate of all of the possible costs involved in writing.)
8. Have you ever been publicly disciplined for any unlawful or unethical actions in your professional career? Which organizations are you regulated by? (Contact these groups to conduct a background check. See Chapter 14)
9. Can I have it in writing? (Ask the advisor to provide you with a written agreement that details the services that will be provided. Keep this document in your files for future reference.)

Involve Other Professionals

It may be helpful to bring one or more of your other professional advisors with you to the second or third meetings with a prospective advisor when you ask those pertinent questions. This serves a couple of purposes. It introduces the new advisor to the current members of your team, and it gives you another professional's perspective on the advisor. Those other professionals may ask some very penetrating questions for your benefit.

Check Them Out

How do you know if an advisor has integrity, is ethical *and* competent? When asked, the majority of advisors agree that getting and checking references is an important part of the process. Not only should you ask for references, but also go the extra mile and call them. You should ask questions such as:

1. What were/are your objectives?
2. How does the advisor help you meet those objectives?
3. Does the advisor put you into investments that you are comfortable with?
4. (For conservative investors) Did the advisor put you in anything that was too risky for your tolerance level?
5. What do you like about the advisor? Why?
6. Give me an idea of the things that the advisor does for you to service your account.

7. Are there any extraordinary or unusual things that the advisor has done that have made you a raving fan?
8. How often are you in contact with your advisor?
9. Have you given the advisor's name to any of your friends and family as referrals?
10. What are a couple of things that you wish the advisor would do better?

In Conclusion

Now that you know how to find an advisor, read the next two chapters to find out what you should expect to hear from an advisor during the initial meeting.

◆◆◆

Pluta on Integrity

"Building trust with a client comes by a steadfast adherence to an ethical and moral code. Lately, much has been made of unethical practices pursued as a shortcut to success. The irony lies in the fact that actual success, as opposed to the masquerade of temporary success, cannot be achieved without the highest adherence to the code.

Our fiduciary role necessitates a paternalistic view that goes further than the classic oath of 'do no harm' and adds a protective element that does not sell, but advises. It does not dictate, but explains. It does not mystify, but simplifies. Not because someone said that it should be so, but because it must be so.

No calling is more noble than to dedicate ones life to enriching others lives. There's simply nothing else that delivers such incredible success by way of client experience, retention, referrals and personal job satisfaction. We bring the client and their unique situation together and find harmonic solutions that appear to be obvious now, but were elusive prior. In an area of immense confusion coupled with information overload, the relationship is at its best when we seek simplicity on the other side of complexity, while the code is adhered to effortlessly. The vow is to provide the best possible service to the best of our ability and enrich the lives of our clients."

Craig Pluta
Co-founder, ReAct! Group
First VP, Ziegler Investment Services Group

Chapter 6

Identifying Long-Term Goals and Objectives

A significant part of preparing to find an advisor is deciding what you want the advisor to do for you. This decision is based on what you want your money to do for you and your family as well.

The previous chapter provided a series of steps that you can take to find an appropriate advisor or advisory team to help you meet your overall financial goals and objectives. But that assumes you have a clear idea of exactly what you want your money to do for you. As previously stated, without a clear understanding of what you want and need for your financial future, it is impossible to determine whether a particular advisor can assist you in attaining it.

Knowing what you want your money to do for you and your family goes far beyond typical goals and objectives such as, "I want my money to grow," "I want to retire comfortably and travel around the world," and "We want our daughter to go to an Ivy League school." While these are worthwhile goals, they are much too vague and don't encompass the full realm of possibilities. Remember, financial goals are usually a means to an end.

It is important to give thought to numerous personal, family and financial issues before even meeting with an advisor. A good advisor will help you further identify and define your goals and then help you construct a plan to achieve them. But it all starts with you knowing where you want to go. Metaphorically, you are the owner of a ship. You decide where to go, and the captain and the crew (financial and professional advisors) determine how to get you there.

It is also important to do some contingency planning; that is, allow for unexpected obstacles or situations. While it would be impossible to list all of the things that may happen over the years to come, here are a few common occurrences that must be considered. After all, any one of the following could happen to you, a loved one, or any individual you know.

- Car accidents. Approximately 40,000 people will die in automobile accidents this year and tens of thousands of others will be severely and permanently injured.
- Home accidents that temporarily or permanently disable hundreds of thousands of people each year. (It could be something as simple as slipping in the shower.)
- Heart attacks and strokes affect large numbers of people.
- Cancer
- Alzheimer's disease affects large percentages of the elderly.
- Prolonged stock market melt-downs
- Economic, social, political instability
- Terrorist activity
- Bankruptcy
- Corporate buy-out or corporate failure

A good advisor will help you plan for contingencies and recommend investment strategies that insulate you from unexpected events and recurring events such as bear markets.

Therefore, it is important to look at your personal, family, and financial situations from many angles. Considering the "outcome of the outcome" is another way to look at it. For example, if you contribute money to a charitable foundation, how might that affect the education you had hoped to provide your great grandchildren or, perhaps, your own finances sometime in the future?

Cella Quinn of Cella Quinn Investment Services feels clients need to wait until they are in their advanced senior years before giving much money away. She fears the economy may go through some bad years and that clients will need the money they are now donating. She knows a number of people who have given money to churches and/or charities and who could now use it.

"When the money is gone, it's gone," she says.

She advises clients, who are in the wealth-building stage, not to get infatuated with the tax write-off. "Remember, for every dollar you give away, you only get to write–off about one-third of that. Giving away $1 to get 30 cents back is no way to build wealth—you can't make it up in volume."

"Build as big a nest egg as you can. I think this economy is in a precarious situation," she says. A student of economic history, Quinn says that whenever there is an economic crisis, those with wealth may lose some of the money; however they live better during the crisis and they come out much better in the end.

A variation of the "outcome of the outcome" question is to determine how your legacy plans will be furthered if you contribute additional money to a particular cause. Also, how might it affect your tax situation?

The Discovery

To help with the process of identifying more precisely what you want your money to accomplish, many advisors provide prospective clients with a detailed questionnaire that allows them to carefully answer a series of questions prior to an initial meeting. The questionnaire has two distinct parts – financial and non-financial.

The financial portion of the questionnaire contains questions you might expect. It asks about your assets, liabilities, income, and expenditures. You'll be asked to bring the last three to five years of tax returns with you as well as other important documents, such as statements showing your portfolio, any estate documents, wills, trusts, insurances, etc. Copies of your pension or profit-sharing plan also are important pieces of information. Basically, you are going to get a thorough financial physical. You should be asked numerous questions about potential expenses, such as long-term care for a parent or special projects that you may wish to financially contribute to.

Before discussing the non-financial questions, it is extremely important to highlight a couple of important points. Any representative or advisor you select should want to look at your tax returns. If a representative or advisor doesn't even request to see your tax return, you are probably dealing with someone at the low end of the education and capabilities continuums. While there may be exceptions, they are few and very far between.

Tom Gau of Oregon Pacific Financial Advisors says, "If someone does not even look at your tax return, it is my opinion that they cannot do their job properly. It's that simple. What about capital loss carryover? What about stepped-up cost basis? Other issues that I look at [on a tax return] are net unrealized appreciation or losses."

Here are some additional questions for your consideration:

- What circumstances have motivated you to seek advice and counsel?
- Why is your money important to you?
- What are your primary financial goals and objectives?
- What are your personal, family, business goals and objectives?
- Where would you like to be five years from now? What is your time horizon to get there? What percentage of assets do you envision being allocated to each goal?
- What is your financial and emotional ability to handle risk?

Advisors ask numerous questions in order to truly understand your needs. They ask questions about finances, family, beliefs, needs, etc. – all with the goal of better understanding their clients and, therefore, being able to create better financial solutions. Both parties need to see the "big picture." Consider the following metaphor from a famous story that originated in India.

The Wisest Person

A king wanted to find out who the wisest person was in his kingdom. He had six of the smartest people in the land brought to him for a test. He had all of them blindfolded and brought into a room where there was an elephant—an animal no one was familiar with. He asked the blindfolded men to touch the elephant, and then figure out what the animal looked like based on what they felt with their hands.

After touching the elephant, one described the animal as a huge fan, for he had touched the ear. Another described it as the trunk of a tree, for he had touched the leg. The third compared it to a wall, having touched the elephant's side. The fourth, touching the tusk, thought the elephant was like a spear. The fifth, who touched the tail, described it as a rope. The sixth disagreed with them all and described the elephant as a powerful vine, for he had touched the trunk.

The king came to realize that each was right and each was wrong for they had extrapolated the look of the entire animal based upon touching just one part.

Isn't that the challenge for many investors? For example, the insurance professional oversees the insurance portion of a financial plan, the CPA takes care of the tax portion, the financial advisor manages the portfolio, and the attorney watches over the estate plan. This mix of advisory professionals overseeing an investor's financial plan can result in a jumble of uncoordinated ideas and tactics.

Your total profile is a compilation of many aspects of your life. You should have a chief advisor who can view the whole person—your finances, dreams, values, charitable interests, family goals, etc.—in order to get the big picture. This advisor can then orchestrate the efforts of other professionals to help you achieve your dreams. This is a more "holistic" or comprehensive wealth management approach.

After all, you are more than a businessperson, spouse, and parent. Each person is so much more than those labels that are filled in on job applications and resumes. Everyone is an "elephant"—that is, we all have many different attributes that make up our whole person.

The high-level advisor knows how to bring the appropriate professionals together to comprehensively meet the needs of their clients. This advisor also has the sophistication to orchestrate the talents of those other professionals. This talent is both rare and valuable, which is why high-level advisors ask you so many detailed questions.

Comprehensive Planning Issues

In the case study to the right (*Your Vision*), Michael Searcy explains that there are four areas of traditional financial planning that should be addressed. These areas are: estate planning, insurance analysis, financial freedom, otherwise known as retirement, and investment management. He discusses each of these areas with the client to determine where they stand, what planning they already have in place, what they wish to accomplish, and what they believe the final result of their planning should be.

YOUR VISION

Michael Searcy of Searcy Financial Services says his team believes it is really important to fully understand a client's vision for their life and know that they have addressed all the various components of the client's vision. According to Mike, "There is no point in planning if it doesn't address the big-picture issues associated with a client's life."

Here are some of the additional questions that he asks prospective clients:

- If you could create the perfect lifestyle or existence for your family, what would it be like?
- If you could change things in the world, your community, and your country, what would they be?
- How do you feel about faith and religion?
- How do you feel about your heirs?
- Is your spouse good at handling money and making business or financial decisions?
- What is preventing or delaying you from pursuing those things that make the best use of your time, talent, and resources?

Mike and his team also ask a host of general questions such as "Tell me what is going on in your life so we can help you identify landmines that can possibly be avoided. To guide you through the landmines, we need to know where all of them are."

The Client Risk Profile

Mike and his team also provide examples of hypothetical portfolios that are invested in various asset allocations. "By doing this, we can show them the upside potential as well as the downside risk of loss. This allows us to determine their risk tolerance. This also helps us understand how they react to significant shifts so we can alter our approach to a method that they are comfortable with," he says.

Client Satisfaction and Personalities

They also ask simple questions such as a client's preference on communications—do they prefer e-mail, faxes, snail mail, phone calls, etc.? Whom should they be communicating with (i.e., husband or wife)? "If one of them is a procrastinator and the other gets things handled immediately, then we know whom to contact if we need immediate action."

"We also try to find out what kinds of things help them make a decision. Some clients are extremely analytical and want to read each prospectus cover to cover along with any additional analysis they can get their hands on. We try to make sure that we send those clients additional information up front so that they feel like they are making an educated decision."

"We ask our clients, what needs to happen in order for you to say in 10 or 15 years, 'Hiring Searcy Financial Services was one of the best decisions we have ever made.'"

Similarly, the other advisors interviewed ask clients a series of detailed questions. Some of them use questionnaires, others a blank piece of paper.

Bill Baker of William Baker & Associates, Inc. uses a block diagram to better understand the client's family tree. He wants to know who's who and where everybody fits on the tree. He'll ask questions about inter-relationships, if any of the family members are estranged, whether there are any issues with children (drugs, motivation, etc.), and how the dynamics of the family work.

For each member on the block diagram, there are questions such as "Will there be any special financial obligations for this person? Will there be any windfalls expected from this family member?"

"Going through that family tree is extremely informative," Bill says.

And, the process goes even deeper to include questions about: insurance coverage; family and other business interests; status of estate planning and associated documentation; assets and ownership; and tax control techniques the client might be using. Many discoveries are made using this walk-through of the very simple, family-tree block diagram. Much of that information will then flow right into the preparation of the financial plan.

Says Bill, "I also explore family legacy issues. Some clients feel they have already provided for their children and have no interest in leaving them more. Others are very interested in bequeathing the assets to their heirs. In either case, it opens the discussion to charitable giving approaches and/or alternative ways of dividing their estate among heirs. Follow-up discussions might include an estate attorney."

When looking at a financial plan, the advisor needs to know about good, bad, and deteriorating relationships.

The advisors in this book all emphasize that their success in helping their clients hinges on obtaining this type of critical information. This fact-finding truly differentiates them from their competitors and is vital to helping clients identify, define, and achieve their financial goals.

Things to Consider

The questions below are derived from two sources[1] and are designed to assist investors with important issues prior to choosing an investment adviser. Keep in mind that not all types of financial advisors will ask you these or similar questions because their business focus may be different. Nevertheless, it is important that you have thought about these questions. You can refine and crystallize your answers later.

***Values*—**What principles, values, and virtues are important to you? Why? How and with whom do you intend to share them? (Some clients may want to share with their immediate family, others, the world.) How do you wish to be remembered?

***Family/Community/Country/World*—**What things in your family, community, country, or world, would you like to change, preserve, protect or re-establish? How important is this to you, and how do you intend to accomplish this? What resources will be employed to assist you?

***People*—**Who in your life do you most want to impact? Why and how? What are the most effective ways to do so? What procedures do you have in place or intend to put into place to help ensure that your wishes are fulfilled?

***Approaches and Vehicles*—**Do you want "hands-on" control? How do you want to help other people and organizations (community, charity, political) with similar pursuits?

***Resources*—**How much time, effort, and money are you willing or able to devote to the accomplishment of your goals? What are your priorities? What additional internal and external resources can you enlist to support your efforts?

***Support Resources*—**Who can you turn to for help, support, or guid-

[1]*The Mega Producers: Secrets of Financial Services Superstars to Lead You to the Top* by Steven Drozdeck (Dearborn Trade Publishing, 2003) and *The Wright EXIT Strategy: Wealth—How to Create It, Keep It, and Use It* by Bruce Wright (Sammi Press, 1997). 800-729-5791. Free workbook is available.

in the dynamic execution of your life goals? How will they help you? What else can they do? Why are they doing it?

By thinking about what you want before you search for an advisor, you significantly increase the probability of finding the right advisor to help you realize your goals and aspirations.

> To effectively work with a financial advisor, you must be able to tell the advisor specifically what you want.

George Jackson of Jackson Retirement Planning was the CFO of two public companies before becoming a financial advisor. He says that it takes time to build a client-advisor relationship and for people to truly realize that he and his team really care about them as individuals. He makes a key point: "Over time the relationship becomes even more significant. The better I get to know the client, the better I can serve them."

George adds that clients hire him because they want a life. They want him to manage all the complexities of taxes, investments, and estate planning. "So we essentially become a one-stop shop where they can basically hire, on a part-time basis, a chief financial officer for their family. I'll tell clients that they are the owner of the team. I am their coach. I'm going to put this team together and hire the right players. But it's their money, so they make the final decisions. In designing a plan, I'm talking in terms of being an architect. The client really drives what they want, [just like] the architect, through his knowledge of construction, is able to construct houses that are financially sound or solidly built," he says.

VALUABLE ADVICE

George Jackson provides two examples of how being able to communicate effectively with his clients has allowed him to solve complex problems:

Example #1: A client has a large estate. Estate and income taxes could reduce the value of the estate by about $3 million and must be paid within nine months of death. George says, "Rather than deplete the inherited IRA by $3 million, one way to handle the problem is to set up a life insurance policy inside an irrevocable trust to add liquidity."

However, in this case, the client did not want life insurance and wanted to make sure that his children would receive the money over their lifetime. So, George, through a qualified estate planning attorney, set up a private foundation that would handle the distribution. The estate tax would be reduced because the money was going into a private foundation and the children would receive money throughout their lives via an Inherited IRA that would make payments over the children's life expectancies.

Example #2: In this situation George had a client who recently had a trust revised. His former broker never retitled the accounts which were still in the name of the old trusts. Had something happened to the client, the improperly titled accounts would have had devastating consequences.

George notes that when he meets with prospective clients, he often finds three or more major flaws that the client never even knew existed.. Rather than criticize the other advisor, George feels that his job is to help. In such situations he says, "This is what needs to get done. Let's just do it."

In these summarized versions, you can see how George had to use his extensive knowledge of investment, tax, and legal strategies to solve a complex problem.

In Conclusion

Before looking for an advisor, it is wise to determine what goals and objectives you want the advisor to help you achieve. Once you know what you want, it is easier to find someone who can help you accomplish it.

High-level advisors have the experience and knowledge to structure a customized solution to fit your specific needs. In today's complex society, it is too easy for a client or less highly trained representative to make a mistake that could result in devastating consequences. Hence, when it comes to advisor selection, it is important to choose wisely.

Searcy on Integrity

"In work and in life, to get the best results, you must engage the most excellent people. I have learned that the most excellent people are also people of high integrity. Integrity means doing the right thing even when the price is painful or one's personal interest is at risk. It means doing the right thing even when you are certain that no one is looking, and you could not possibly get caught should you choose *not* to do the right thing. It also means doing the right thing even when you are sure there will not be a reward or you will not receive any credit for your actions.

During the 30 years I have served as a financial advisor, I have continuously endeavored to:

(1) achieve excellence in the level and quality of service that we provide to our clients,

(2) meet clients wherever they are and to help them get to where they want to be,

(3) faithfully pursue knowledge and grow both personally and professionally,

(4) always deal with honesty and integrity in every situation.

Life is full of choices and a person of high integrity will choose to put their clients' best interests ahead of their own."

Michael J. Searcy, ChFC, CFP™, AIF™
President
Searcy Financial Services, Inc.

Chapter 7

RESEARCH and REVIEW: The First Meeting

PROCESS: Research

- Studious, systematic investigation or inquiry to ascertain, uncover, or assemble facts; used as a basis for conclusions or the formulation of theory.
- To do research on or for.

Your initial meeting with a financial advisor is very important. It allows each party to get to know and assess each other. It determines whether you'll have subsequent meetings and can set the tone for the remainder of the relationship.

It is important that you feel comfortable with the financial advisor on a personal level and that the advisor feels comfortable with you. After all, you may be working with each other for years to come, and that relationship will probably extend to other members of your family. You must be able to trust each other. You must feel that the advisor will look after you and your interests.

During the first meeting you want to get to know each other and get a feel for compatibility.

One of the things that Mike Piershale has found most rewarding is helping couples in instances where one person is handling all the finances and the other finds it distasteful. On several occasions, couples in this situation have elected him to become their financial advisor out of concern that the financially savvy spouse may pass away first. They gain the peace of mind that someone they have confidence in—who is knowledgeable and has their best interests at heart—will be there to help the inexperienced partner with the financial affairs. Mike states, "I have found that nine out of ten times, in cases like these, it is the husband handling the finances. In many cases, his wife has no experience or interest in finances. It is a common problem that the man handling the finances passes away before his wife, and she has to deal with financial matters that she's inexperienced with, while going through the loss of her husband. We make this transition very smooth. I have told many couples that in a case such as this, they should develop a relationship with a financial advisor while they are both able to do so."

The Elements of Trust

Throughout this book we have referenced some of the elements of trust, but the word "trust" is impossible to precisely define because the definition will vary for each individual. We've looked at tools such as the trust continuum and added in a few additional pieces of the puzzle. In this section, we look at trust from a compatibility angle, and offer a number of questions that you can ask current and potential advisors. These questions will provide insight into who these advisors are and the value they offer you.

Compatible Investment Philosophy and Approach

An advisor's investment philosophy or approach should make sense to you. What are they helping you accomplish? Does it mesh with your objectives? While investment philosophies and approaches are discussed more fully in Chapters 10 and 13, it is important to have a general feel for what you are looking for prior to meeting with your first advisor candidate as described in the previous chapter. If not, you run the risk of a financial representative asking some general questions and then jumping to an inappropriate investment conclusion. Investors who are not financially sophisticated might actually agree with the representative's misguided assessment.

Brian Puckett of Brian Puckett Retirement Advisors uses a baseball analogy when he says his goal is to hit singles and doubles, not necessarily home runs. As Brian says, "We're not going to be right for the client who is trying to shoot the lights out trying to hit home runs with their investments. We have a very disciplined process and take a somewhat conservative approach to managing money. I think that we appeal to someone who is sensitive to tax issues because we have a fair amount of education and experience in areas like tax planning, estate planning, and tax-wise wealth management."

If you were to choose Brian Puckett Retirement Advisors you should relate to the previous sentence on a gut level. If not, and you are substantially more aggressive, for instance, you would continue your search for another investment advisor.

But …

An extremely important point must be made here. Many investors "do not know what they don't know" and make a series of erroneous assumptions about what they want/need their money to do for them and about investments in general. Media influence, peers, and unconscious, unrealistic expectations often cause people to want things that would be counter-productive to their overall financial and emotional health. For example, during the technology craze of the 1990s, millions of investors threw unwarranted amounts of money into technology stocks in the unrealistic hope that they would make a market killing. Otherwise conservative investors became high-risk speculators because their actions were based on a false premise and unbridled hopes.

Other investors want to be so conservative that they think CDs are the most logical investment for their money. Their fear of the stock market (or, more likely, lack of understanding) may prevent them from considering equities for the growth component necessary to beat inflation. They may not realize that their failure to include equities actually places them in a higher risk category.

As a third and final example, many people may be astute with respect to investments but don't have sufficient tax or legal knowledge to accomplish their overriding goals and may assume certain things "that just ain't so," much to their detriment.

In the three previous examples it is the function and obligation of the advisor to ask penetrating questions, go beyond the stated needs, and educate the investor to the more appropriate approaches. Investors who are willing to learn are "coachable" or "teachable" and become excellent clients. High-level advisors often choose not to work with people who cannot be taught or who refuse to be taught. Unfortunately, those who cannot see the light often start working with financial salespeople who will generally sell them what they want, rarely considering the long-term ramifications.

Here is another "but." The above is not to say that investors are always wrong and advisors are always right. Such would be a gross misstatement. If someone has really thought through what they want their money to do for them, the advisor's questions usually refine the objectives. Advisors often help people come to new understandings of the purposes and capabilities of money, but they also must realize that it is the investor's money. The advisor's purpose is to help people identify, define, and achieve their goals within the advisor's skill sets and business model.

The point is, an advisor traverses a fine line when investing someone else's money. There are a lot of choices and alternatives that must be considered. The final decision, of course, is always in your hands. You ultimately choose the advisor to work with–one, hopefully, who is compatible with you on many levels.

In your selection process, search for advisors who are specialists in the areas you need. Beware of financial representatives who try to be all things to all people. No one individual can do everything–too much knowledge is required. Firms with multiple advisors and numerous people trained in a variety of financial disciplines have a much better chance of helping you than the lone representative pretending that he is equally competent in all areas. This is why it is important to choose an advisor who has a strong team – whether internal or external–as is described in Chapter 12.

It is difficult to determine a professional's competency, however, unless you examine their educational degrees and business reputations.

Personal and Personnel Compatibility

While you may not be able to judge a person's competency with 100 percent accuracy, you can get a feel for them as people–whether they seemed concerned about you or whether they put you through a cookie-cutter analysis. Did they ask you a lot of questions (as described in the next chapter) and actually listen to the answers? Did they answer your questions and make sure that you understood the answers? All of these factors allow you to intuitively know whether this advisor is right for you. Remember that this is "the honeymoon stage." If they are not making a good impression on you before you become a client, don't assume that will change later on.

However, don't assume that trust will develop immediately. Brian Puckett says, "Trust isn't just something that just pops up. It happens gradually and it happens over time, and only if you earn it. A financial advisor has got to consistently earn it over and over again. I've found that a person can be the most competent advisor in the world, but if they ever lose sight of the fact that it's all about the client, and if the client senses for a minute that their advisor's agenda is anything other than what the client is trying to accomplish, then the effectiveness of the advice is lost."

Also realize that you may not "click" with an extremely competent advisor just because of personality differences. That's why it's wise to have a range of advisors to choose from.

Brian reminds us that "People don't trust companies or institutions, they trust people. Higher level conversations about goals, objectives, dreams, hopes, fears, etc. occur with another human being."

Account Size Compatibility

You should ask advisors you interview about their long-term business plans, such as how large the organization may be in the next five to 10 years. You don't want to get lost in the shuffle of a large-scale operation.

Also, the size of your account should match the size of other accounts handled by the advisor. For example, you don't want to be someone's biggest client. Why? Because if that advisor only deals with smaller clients (presumably with less demanding needs), that advisor may not have the sophistication level you need. Conversely, if you are one of the advisor's smaller clients, you must question the level of service and attention you will receive. This does not always happen, but it is something to consider.

Experience and Designations

Often, professional designations are proof that the advisor has gone the extra mile to upgrade his or her knowledge and skills. However, just because an advisor has one or more professional designations, doesn't make him or her the best person for the job. Some advisors joke about having so many designations behind their names that it looks like alphabet soup. As you'll see in Chapter 14, different designations infer different skills and competencies. If an advisor does not have the designations needed to help you, he or she should have access to people with the required knowledge. (Chapter 12 includes information on multi-disciplinary teams.)

The First Meeting

The first meeting or interview is the best time for you and an advisor to get to know each other on a personal level and the best time to begin a professional relationship. Hopefully, many of the compatibility questions previously raised will be answered to your satisfaction. During your discussion, the advisor will ask you a lot of questions about your personal goals, financial goals, understanding of the markets, and the names and functions of your other advisors (attorney, accountant, insurance agent).

You can use the "10 Questions to Ask When Choosing a Financial Planner" from Chapter 5 or the questions provided in this chapter as the basis for your questions. In the first and second meeting, expect a lot of give-and-take as you get to know each other.

In addition, you can expect the advisor to:

- Explain his or her financial planning and/or in investment process
- Discuss reasonable expectations regarding service, market returns, etc.
- Explain costs of service and the limits of the services provided
- Provide written materials that reflect any agreement and projected costs
- Describe office team members and any other strategic relationships with other professionals
- Introduce you to the other team members with whom you will be interacting
- Describe his or her qualifications

Criteria for Selecting an Advisor

Each advisor in this book offers some insight into how to evaluate a potential advisor. You'll note that the next five questions are ways of asking, "Is this the person or team that I am willing to entrust my future to?"

1. ***Is the advisor adding value?*** The advisor should fill a particular need that you have. Ask each advisor what "value added[1]" they offer and what differentiates them from their competitors. Those people who respond with a "sales pitch" are obviously trying to sell you on their services and probably ought to be avoided. However, don't confuse enthusiasm with selling. High-level advisors are very proud of what they can do for you and what they have accomplished for others. You'll probably hear that sense of pride in their voice. On the other hand, you would be wise to avoid someone who tries to have you sign on the dotted line, or make an immediate investment decision, or has a solution before they've done the diagnosis.
2. ***Is the system right for me?*** Most advisors have a process that does two things very well: attracts potential clients and repels potential clients. They have defined procedures, investment approaches, service standards and "a way of doing things" that causes like-minded people to be impressed and see the value. Other people may see things differently and search for a system that is more suited to their own tastes. Remember that a system is a set of procedures that specifies how an advisor conducts his or her businesses. Advisors will agree that it is better to have a potential client say "no thanks" than it is for someone to become a client and then be disappointed with something.
3. ***Do we think alike?*** During your initial conversation both you and the advisor will have the opportunity to get to know each other. The advisor wants to determine if you're "coachable"—that is, willing to be helped, guided, and taught—or if you will insist on things that the advisor either cannot deliver or are not in alignment with his or her business approach. You must make sure that the advisor is not so rigid that flexibility and customization to your unique needs is precluded.
4. ***Do they have the right experience?*** The more objectives you have, the more problems you want to solve, and the more experience and depth you need from an advisor. It is suggested that you choose an advisor with a minimum of five years' experience, and preferably more than 10 years. A sad fact within the financial services industry is that the vast majority of people who start as financial representatives leave the business within five years.

[1] "Value-added," a term often used within the financial services industry, describes why you should do business with that person or firm. In financial industry conferences, attendees are told to identify what makes them unique/different/better than others who theoretically have the same knowledge and available investments.

Michael Searcy of Searcy Financial Services goes one step further by recommending that the advisor be more than 30 years old and has, at bare minimum, at least 10 years of experience as a financial advisor. Says Mike, "One of the problems in the industry today is that the person who used to sell you life insurance or mutual funds, or did your banking or tax returns is now a "financial planner" or advisor. Make sure that the advisor has 10 years of relevant experience providing comprehensive planning."

5. ***Do they ask the right questions?*** An excellent way to determine if an advisor will add value, thinks the way you do, and is someone you can work with, is based on what questions they ask you and how they ask them. In the previous chapter, we suggested that you spend time answering questions about what money means to you and your family. Also, we discussed how top advisors will conduct in-depth interviews, probing into your needs and goals. If an advisor doesn't ask you in-depth questions, you probably shouldn't work with him or her. One of worst things an advisor can do is to quickly and conveniently place you in a pre-set mental category and offer you a cookie-cutter solution to investing. Stay away from this financial assembly-line approach.

Things Investors Do Wrong When Selecting an Advisor

Before providing additional questions that you can ask the advisor, here is a list of common mistakes people make when choosing an advisor. This list will help make the questions that you ask more meaningful.

Michael Searcy offers the following advice when it comes to choosing an advisor.

- Avoid selecting an advisor based on personality. Personalities have absolutely nothing to do with competency and integrity. There are a large number of high-powered salespeople who have been taught to use their powerful personalities to persuade people to follow their ideas. Beware of over-enthusiasm.
- Avoid choosing advisors based solely on proximity. There are a number of outstanding advisors who work with clients throughout the world. Just because someone is located down the street from you, doesn't necessarily mean that they are the best option for you.

Bill Baker of William Baker & Associates identifies the following errors in advisor selection:

- Ill-defined or unrealistic expectations of an advisor. [Unrealistic expectations include: attaining specific investment returns, expecting advisors to violate their own specific disciplines, demanding unreasonable amounts of service, etc]
- Not asking appropriate questions to determine the qualifications and experience of the advisor. [Questions are provided throughout the

book and in the next section of this chapter. Just sitting back and listening to an advisor is not as effective as engaging the advisor in dialogue.]

- Investors who chase hype or performance promises are usually fooling themselves. [If it sounds too good to be true, it usually is. Investment returns are a direct result of the risk assumed. Lower risks offer lower returns. Anyone that offers you higher returns than the 'norm' is asking you to assume higher risks than the 'norm.']
- Investors that go for the lowest bid are usually going to end up dissatisfied. The industry is very competitive and the lowest bid will often provide the lowest results and personal service.

One of the most common mistakes made by an investor is to switch advisors merely because someone is a friend of a friend, or "knows somebody who ..." While it is human nature to trust the word of a friend, it often doesn't make sense in this context.

Cella Quinn of Cella Quinn Investment Services tells of situations in which the "old boy's network" comes into play. She says that wealthy people are surrounded by accountants and attorneys who'll say to them, "I play golf with this guy and he's really good. You should work with him rather than your current advisor." Too often the investor will change advisors without doing their own due diligence [Author's Note: Cella's comment reflects a common industry problem of switching advisors merely based on someone else's opinion. There may be justification to exploring other options, but do your homework! The other problem with taking someone's advice, for example, to switch to his or her "golf buddy," is that he or she has an interest in helping out that buddy. Your friend is probably making the recommendation without knowing what you want/need and whether or not there would be a good fit.]

Other typical mistakes investors make include: (Note that some previous points are reiterated for your convenience.)

- Choosing a personal friend or family member. (This is a variation of the old-boy network that Cella describes, but carries the added pressure of family ties.) If your brother is a stockbroker at a large firm, you may feel obligated to let him manage your account. You may even be under "family pressure" to do so. Of course, after doing your due diligence you may find that he is the best person for the job. But don't automatically assume that a relative or friend is a good advisor. You must decide if that person is the best one available to manage your investments. Is that person a highly trained, credentialed, experienced money manager or financial planner? Does that expertise extend to the specific style of investing you need?
- Choosing an advisor based upon the firm they are associated with.

We've previously commented that the financial services industry spends a tremendous amount of money on advertising and sales promotions. Just look at all those television commercials and print advertisements boasting fantastic slogans that you are constantly exposed to. Those commercials cost a lot of money. When you visit one of those firms, you are assigned to the next available representative -- and don't assume that all their representatives are equally qualified. Don't fall for the hype and become another number within the huge conglomerate.

- Visiting with only one or two advisors before making a selection. The general advice is to interview at least three to five advisors.
- Not being equipped with formulated answers about the purpose and meaning of money in your own life. Without giving this some thought you run the risk of choosing a financial representative who sounds the best rather than the advisor who is best for you.
- Not identifying specific needs that you may have and, therefore, not finding someone who can address those needs. (See an example in the accompanying case study presented by Chris Doughty.)
- Not allocating enough time to do the job.
- Procrastinating.

IN SEARCH OF EXCELLENCE

Chris Doughty of of the ReAct! Group relates an interesting story about a man who had visited numerous advisors in search of the answer to some key financial questions he had.

The man was attending a seminar that Chris was conducting, and during a break Chris asked him if he could help him. The man gruffly answered, that he didn't know. Chris invited him to visit him at his office and then resumed speaking at the seminar.

A few weeks later Chris visited the man's office and discovered that the man had a question regarding net unrealized appreciation and that he had posed his question to at least nine other advisors and received only a "deer-in-the-headlight look" from each of them. Chris knew the answer because he and his partner, Craig Pluta, had decided early in their partnership to become true experts in retirement planning; therefore, he was able to give the man a thorough answer. The man was pleasantly surprised.

He and Chris then discussed some ideas regarding charitable remainder trusts and giving options, with Chris providing comprehensive answers and powerful strategies. As Chris says, "All of a sudden he turned from this rough, 'I'm not sure why we're talking' [attitude] to a good friend. Since then he has given us 19 referrals."

Chris explains that the question on net unrealized appreciation was both a test for the advisors the man posed it to and a desire to learn more so that he wouldn't make any foolish, potentially disastrous decisions regarding his highly appreciated company stock.

Chris helped him diversify his holdings, make numerous charitable contributions, and dramatically improve his tax situation. Until he met Chris, the man thought himself a great investor—only to realize that it was the bull market that made him brilliant.

As an interesting aside, the man didn't realize that he needed help until he met Chris because he assumed that the other nine representatives he had met were representative of the entire industry. In a sense he was right. The other nine were "typical" advisors.

25 Questions to Ask an Advisor

Bill Baker and Michael Searcy offer some additional, excellent questions for you to ask.

1. How is the advisor compensated?
2. Are there any conflicts of interest?
3. Has a regulatory body ever cited them for disciplinary reasons? [As described in Chapter 14, it is easy to look up an advisor's record with different regulatory authorities.]
4. Will they take possession of, or have access to, your assets as part of the arrangement?
5. Do they consider themselves a fiduciary? Why or why not?
6. What investments are available to their clients?
7. What investments and services are *not* available to their clients?
8. What kinds of investments do they utilize in client portfolios (mutual funds, separately managed accounts, index funds, stocks, bonds, etc.)?
9. What is their area of expertise?
10. Do they specialize in any other particular areas?
11. What are their credentials? Experience? Background?
12. Who will handle your needs in other areas?
13. Who can they rely upon for advice in areas outside their specific area(s) or expertise?
14. Who, specifically, do they have professional relationships with?
15. How will they coordinate work with your other advisors?
16. Ask for a copy of their engagement agreement, ADV (see Chapter 14), privacy notice, and any other policies that would affect clients such as proxy statements.

17. What is their target market?
18. What are their business plans over the next five years?
19. What type of support do they have within their offices?
20. Who will be your primary contact at the office?
21. What will they put in writing?
22. Do they have files for each client that includes a written summary of personal goals, needs and objectives? If so, can you see one or two without seeing the name of the individuals involved?
23. Do they have five or six clients who you can call as references?
24. What industry associations are they a member of?
25. Can they describe their ongoing education efforts?

In Conclusion

The first meeting with a potential advisor is critical. This is the time to ask the questions suggested here and to carefully evaluate the responses you receive. The ideas presented here should provide you with additional tools to help in your ultimate choice.

◆◆◆

Quinn on Integrity

"Some clients have been with me since I started in this profession 33 years ago. I have planned with them and helped them as they built their nest egg and put their children through college. I've been with them when they retired and needed additional income. And I have, with great sadness, been with them in their transition out of this life and then I have helped distribute their wealth to loved ones left behind.

That's integrity. People don't stay with you that long and they don't let you help them that much unless you have completely earned their trust."

Cella Quinn, President/CEO
Cella Quinn Investment Services

Chapter 8

OBJECTIVES: Clarification of Your Goals

PROCESS: Objectives

- A goal or purpose, as of a mission or assignment.
- Creation of, or representing, facts or reality without reference to feelings or opinions
- Not prejudiced: unbiased. Detached, fair-minded.

You identified your main objectives in the preparation phase (Chapter 6), which also helped you decide the type of advisor to interview. During the initial meeting, you and the advisor should have learned enough about each other to know whether a second meeting was warranted. During the first meeting, the advisor probably briefly explored your goals, but didn't drill down into them. It is often the second meeting where some or all of your goals are clarified and expanded —forming the basis for your financial strategy.

During this "objective-setting" step of the process, an advisor should help you further identify and refine the goals that you had previously outlined. He or she does this by carefully listening to you and asking additional questions to help refine your objectives and to become quite clear on exactly what he or she must do for you. Some goals may have a leveraging effect on other goals; other goals may be contradictory. Certain goals may even be unrealistic. During this process, the advisor should take good notes to ensure that he or she understands you and to make sure that pertinent information doesn't slip through the cracks. He or she will help categorize those objectives in order of importance. From this information, a plan will be prepared to direct the process toward the attainment of your goals.

During this time an advisor will also help clarify any "fuzzy words" that may be part of your goals. Fuzzy words may have specific meanings for you, but may be unclear to others. Words like "growth," "satisfaction," "contentment," "safety," "protection," and "service" must be specifically defined. For example, what, specifically, does long-term growth mean to you? Is it 20 percent return per year? Is that before or after inflation? Is that growth guaranteed or is there substantial risk involved? Would a growth rate of one percent over inflation be satisfactory? What is the definition of long-term – five, 10, 50 years?

Sometimes people have unrealistic, often unconscious expectations that can't be met. It is best to deal with these early on in the financial planning process than to experience disappointment later on. Expecting a bond to pay 15 percent with a high degree of safety may be an unrealistic expectation if Treasury bonds are only paying three percent.

Advisors should spend time eliciting your conscious and unconscious expectations on future performance and risk. Many have developed some innovative ways to do this and then supplement the information with ongoing communication and education.

Your objectives should be the guiding and driving factor for the entire investment process.

The Total Approach

Once your primary (or guiding) objectives have been identified, the advisor can establish a specific financial or investment plan with its own goals. Investment strategies, products, services, and tactics are the means by which your primary objectives are accomplished. The means (or tools) can be shifted depending upon circumstances, while your primary objectives remain relatively constant and are only changed after a full discussion with the advisor.

Yale Levey of Roseland Financial Group sums up the ultimate role of an advisor when he says, "My practice is a holistic, non-salesy approach focusing on the client. I am sort of a financial doctor. Ultimately, what we really do is pay attention to the client's particular needs, desires, and goals and then address them from a broad perspective. We must listen to everything – listen to their needs as an individual and then take a diagnostic approach and make appropriate recommendations. We find that by helping our clients see the big picture as it relates to their unique situation, we empower them to want to take the necessary actions to accomplish their goals. "

Yale's comment says a lot. First, as financial physicians, advisors must carefully listen to their clients' needs, desires, and goals; they then do a diagnosis and, finally, create a solution. Extending the analogy, we realize that a tremendous amount of knowledge and experience must go into the diagnosis – juggling dozens or hundreds of variables so that the final solution is appropriate for that individual or family.

Eric Hutchinson of Hutchinson/Ifrah Financial Services notes that during the process of uncovering people's needs there are many times when one spouse says to the other, "I didn't realize you felt that way," or "You've never said that to me before." He says, "The process causes people to focus and articulate issues at such a deep level that they often begin talking about things that they've never spoken about or come to grips with as a married couple."

Once everything is brought out into the open, the advisor can create a plan that is specifically designed to meet short-, intermediate-, and long-term goals and needs.

Sometimes the diagnosis is to do "something" quickly before it's too late. On page 70, Eric offers an example of the need to have your affairs in order and to act upon some of the suggestions in this book while you have the opportunity.

The story he relates will help you appreciate the need to get things done. Recall the listing of life's uncertainties from a previous chapter and how we or someone close to us can be affected by any of these tragedies.

What Do You Want to Do with Your Life?

Mark Little of The Freedom Experience® describes an excellent exercise, created by financial services trainer and coach Bill Bachrach called The Quality Of Life Enhancer Exercise™. Mark uses it to help people identify what their real priorities are. "We ask our clients to write down all of the things that are more important than money to them. After they make a complete list, we ask them to determine whether each item is something that can be delegated or not and then to ask themselves questions such as:

- Can I delegate my relationship with my grand children? (The obvious answer is "no.")
- How many hours a week am I spending with my grandchildren and how many hours additional hours per week would I like to spend?
- How important is this to me?

THE TIME IS NOW!

Jim and Judy were referred to Eric Hutchinson, Hutchinson/Ifrah Financial Services. Jim was a general practitioner in a small town in Arkansas and had just suffered a major stroke. He had been in the hospital for about a week while Judy, a nurse, sat by his side coming to grips with the idea that she might lose her husband. He took care of all the finances and she had very little knowledge about their financial affairs.

Fortunately, he snapped out of it without any apparent effects from the stroke. Shortly thereafter, for the first time in their married life, they talked about important goals and resolved to get their affairs in order and to make sure that Judy gained the needed knowledge and skills to carry on in his absence.

Prior to getting anything done in writing, Jim had a second stroke and this put Judy in essentially the same position she had been in a couple of weeks earlier.

It was after the second stroke that they were referred to Eric. Eric met with them in their home. Eric relates, "I talked to them about what was important to them, what my firm did, about our processes, and why it was important to use a systematic approach to ultimately achieve peace of mind about financial matters." Eric learned that Jim had lost his mother and brother the previous year and was the executor of both of their complex estates. He was under tremendous strain due to frustration created by the unwillingness or inability of his bank's trust department to handle the two estates, and his worries for his own health and for Judy's welfare.

Over the next 18 months, Eric helped them with all of their concerns, including the settling of both estates. Everything was in order, all the necessary documents in place, and Judy was now more knowledgeable. At one meeting when there were no more issues, no stone unturned, Judy began to tear up and said, "I'm so grateful that we found you – that you could help us through the process, and for all you have done." Eric recalls "Jim stood up and gave me a very firm, two-handed shake, looked me in the eye and said that he couldn't thank me enough for all I had done for him and Judy."

That was the last time Eric ever saw Jim, because several days later Jim passed away at home in the dining room – the very place he and his wife had first met Eric.

After the funeral, Judy told Eric that she knew that everything was handled and because of that , she was able to focus on being with the children, with the rest of the family, and on honoring Jim's memory. The peace of mind that she had was immeasurable. She also admitted that 18 months earlier she had no idea what Eric was talking about, had no frame of reference, and just didn't get it about financial peace of mind. Judy says, 'Now I get it. If you ever have someone who doesn't get it, you have them call me and I'll explain it to them.'

According to Eric, "This story captures everything that this firm is about and everything about our team as professionals. We are really transforming lives – making a difference in people's lives at a very deep level. It's far more than just managing money or producing a certain rate of return."

- What is my level of commitment to them?

You can see how this can be an enlightening exercise. Another part of the exercise is to ask people to list three activities they would like to do over the next four months that they are not doing as much as they can, should, or like to. They will focus on doing these things between now and the next time Mark meets with them four months from now.

Mark acts somewhat as a coach. At the next meeting he'll ask, "Did you go fishing with your granddaughter like you wanted to?" "Did you delve into a new area of interest?" etc.

Even during market declines, Mark can tell people that they have a well-thought-out plan, and that worrying won't change the plan, so they can focus on values. This is all part of his "Freedom Experience."

Yale Levey of Roseland Financial Group helps families identify their legacy by using a mission statement. Says Yale, "A family mission statement is fantastic because it really helps crystallize the direction the family wants to head in. It helps them to find their purpose and makes it real. They can define how their wealth was obtained, define their beliefs concerning what's important to them – their core values; they can define what they perceive as their responsibility to themselves and to their family members, and define their responsibility to others. If they sign it, it becomes part of the family mission statement or wealth letter of intent. Signing makes it real."

Yale goes on to say that it is important to understand that there are other dimensions to wealth, which include: social wealth (causes and institutions that are important to you); intellectual wealth; and personal wealth (your relationships, emotions, etc.). He observes that financial wealth is just a tool to leverage or enhance those other types of wealth.

He asks his clients, "If you thought about the 10 most important things that have ever happened in your life, how many of them revolve around money or finance? Usually, it's not too many."

What Do You Want to Do with Your Money?

The previous discussions highlight the need to delve into the value or purpose of money. In many cases, it represents the freedom to do what you want, and/or to contribute to whatever causes you are passionate about.

Many of the advisors interviewed for this book work with philanthropies and their clients' families in a variety of ways. Yale Levey discusses this philosophy more indepth on the next page—*The Value of Philanthropy.*

How are Your Assets Currently Positioned?

Depending on the level of service you need, your advisor should conduct a thorough assessment of your current financial position to include your

VALUE OF PHILANTHROPY

Yale Levey of Roseland Financial Group came to the realization that he was in a position to help people in ways he had not yet previously imagined. By introducing his clients to the real benefits —financial, spiritual, social, and emotional— of incorporating philanthropy into their planning , he could leverage his knowledge to create a business designed to provide far more meaning and benefit than simply earning a living. He could also help his clients connect with the more meaningful aspects of what they find important. Financial benefits? Certainly! In addition, they reap all the other intangible benefits derived from adopting a philanthropic cause. Once he decided to focus attention on this area, it gave his business an entirely new meaning.

His approach is that he tells associates and people he's affiliated with that philanthropy is an area he is passionate about.

He communicates the power of three dimensional wealth planning as opposed to one dimensional wealth planning and shows people how, when you skillfully blend your financial, personal and social wealth, you oftentimes will enhance yourself both financially, spiritually and emotionally.

He asks his clients to consider philanthropy as one of their investment planning tools. While this may be a new idea for some clients, Yale finds that many are interested. He says, "Who isn't interested in better serving themselves, their family, and society?"

He has created strategic partnerships with other professionals who have the knowledge, infrastructure and ability to assist him in providing planning options for those clients who are interested.

He has associated with professional organizations to keep himself abreast of industry changes and innovations.

He trains colleagues to better understand the value of what he does and how they can also help their clients and society.

He's a candidate for a Chartered Advisor in Philanthropy designation.

He tries to do a little bit every day to make life better for ev**eryon**e around him.

"My goals for the future are pretty simple and straightforward," Yale says. "I want all my new business relationships to evolve around philanthropy so that I can help people leverage their financial resources to create opportunity and support the efforts of the people, causes, and institutions that are meaningful to them. By doing this, I add a more meaningful dimension to their lives, the lives of those people they are close to, the lives of those people connected to the causes they're passionate about, and, not least of all, to my own life."

current portfolio and how all of your financial assets are allocated. The advisor should ensure that you are properly diversified, have titled your assets properly, have an effective way to monitor your investments, have the correct types and amounts of insurance coverage, and examined any trusts, wills, estate plans, etc. that you currently have.

Also, depending upon his or her specialty, the advisor will develop a number of plans and strategies to get you where you want to be. At each point in the process, he or she should explain the tax, legal, and investment objective of each strategy or tool that he or she recommends from the thousands of options available. Everything should be logical and fit together like pieces of a complex puzzle. Advisors should be willing to explain what they are doing in writing and welcome the opportunity to share their knowledge with you.

Advisors will often call in other experts to assist them, whether they are members of their own staff/firm or outside strategic partners (see Chapter 12) that bring specific skills and expertise to the table. Of course, if possible, they will work with your other current advisors, such as your accountant or attorney, to create a viable course of action.

The individual investments (stocks, bonds, mutual funds, CDs/GICs, etc.) that they and their team may recommend will also be viewed very objectively (as described in Chapters 10 and 13) and monitored carefully to make it is "doing its part" within your overall portfolio and plan. Again, your advisor will be able to explain the specific rationale behind each investment and how it fits within the scheme of things.

In Conclusion

Brian Puckett of Brian Puckett Retirement Advisors sums up the essential ideals that all of these advisors adhere to. He essentially says: "Mr. or Mrs. Client, let's get crystal clear about where you are right now. You are at point "A" with your assets, liabilities, cash flow, employment situation, etc. Let's do a simple inventory process. But more importantly, where do you want to go? Where is your point "B"? What are your hopes? What are your dreams? What are the opportunities that you see that you want to capitalize on, and what are some of the dangers that you want to make sure we protect against? Who are the people you love and that you want to receive this capital that you worked so hard to accumulate? Then we can work together to devise a logical plan, based on reasonable expectations, to make all that happen as efficiently and as cost and tax effective as possible."

Your objectives ultimately determine your course of action. When you are clear about the value or purpose of money in your life, you create a series of over-riding objectives that guide your advisor when shaping your financial plan and strategies. The advisor, in turn, has specific objectives or functions for each of the financial strategies and vehicles that are used.

◆◆◆

Jackson on Integrity

"Integrity is what makes me whole. Honesty is the only way it works in building the long-term client relationships I desire. Trust is not given by clients, I have to earn it every day by truthfully and consistently delivering on what I promise. Dishonesty damages relationships, destroys credibility, and is detrimental to one's health. Honesty is the best policy and the only policy, there is no other way in business or in life."

George P. Jackson, CPA, CFA, CFP®, CLU, ChFC
President
Jackson Retirement Planning, Inc.

Chapter 9

COMMUNICATION: A Dual Responsibility

PROCESS: Communication

- The act of communicating; exchange of ideas, conveyance of information.
- That which is communicated, as a letter or message.

Communication between you and your advisor is the key to a successful and strong long-term relationship. You should know how your investment plan is working, what the advisor is doing, how money managers are performing, and what mid-course corrections may be necessary. In addition, you must remember to inform your advisor of any changes in your personal or financial situation, such as divorce, tax liabilities, and changes of financial objective.

Communication, in one form or another, occurs at every stage of the relationship and actually begins with the marketing materials that advisors distribute to clients and prospective clients. The materials convey, among other information, a mission statement, business approaches, and services available. Reputation and service quality is communicated through referrals and references, by how a receptionist answers the phone, and the appearance of the office. Advisors should go to great lengths to ensure they project a clear picture of themselves and what they do.

Many high-level advisors have "relationship managers" or "communication specialists" who periodically contact each client for updates while, at the same time, updating the client about economic, market, and portfolio changes. The advisor and/or relationship manager meets with each client, depending on the size and complexity of the account, either quarterly, semi-annually, or annually. In addition, they often send out regular written updates or newsletters. Educational seminars are another component of the communication process.

An Understanding

From the advisor's perspective, it is not only important that the client is told about the communication process, but that the client *understands* the essence of the process.

It is important that the advisor be able to describe the process and for clients to be able to say they are comfortable with it. This includes everything from how the portfolio is constructed to establishing reasonable expectations and how periodic reviews are handled to what types of services are provided and why.

Communication is one of the essential ingredients to a successful relationship – whether it is a personal or a business relationship.

Communication between advisor and client occurs in many forms and takes place at each stage of the relationship. For example, the initial meeting, where the advisor provides information regarding services offered. You can expect to receive various pieces of information that reinforce the key concepts presented.

Some advisors provide clients a "service commitment letter" that spells out what their clients can expect from the team. Such letters provide specificity and hold the advisor accountable.

Other items commonly provided at the first or second meeting include a fee schedule, client references, capability statements, articles or white papers exploring different aspects of investing, personnel charts and explanations of duties each team member performs, and who to contact for your various needs. The advisor should also hold periodic follow-ups that provide you and the advisor with necessary updates (one of this chapter's topics). In addition, he or she should keep you informed through educational meetings and conferences, performance reports, and newsletters and periodicals.

At the initial meeting, you and the advisor should be exploring your goals and objectives. In addition, you should be communicating with each other regarding investment choices and what constitutes reasonable expectations for service, investment performance, etc. Expect the advisor to take copious notes at each meeting; those notes should become part of your permanent file.

[Author's Note: Copious notes in a permanent file (electronic or otherwise) are a hallmark of high-level advisors. Working with numerous clients – each with different needs and issues – requires a note-taking system that is more elaborate than one's memory.]

Periodic Follow-up Meetings

The advisors interviewed for this book contact each of their client at least annually, if not semi-annually or quarterly.They also call them when life changes occur. During those meetings they review and update the financial plan, discuss what is new in the market, consider any changes in their client's personal, business, and financial circumstances, and generally make sure that everything is on track.

George Jackson of Jackson Retirement Planning always asks two key questions whenever he meets a client for a periodic meeting.

1. "How's your health?" because if there is a major change in health then we may need to revise your plans. Changes in your own health or that of a family member (or business partner) can cause major shifts in your thinking and your needs. Some parts of your plan may be accelerated, others postponed, at least temporarily.
2. "How is your cash flow?" The answer opens up an entire discussion that may include changes in employment prospects, balloon payments that must be made, unexpected expenses, corporate bonuses, etc. Any of these, and a host of others, can cause a shift in strategy.

Of course, these are not the only questions George asks during his regular meetings with clients. The discussions often delve into many areas such as educational needs, philanthropic wishes, etc.

Since George is a CPA his separate CPA firm prepares his financial planning clients' tax returns as part of his services and, therefore, is quite aware of their tax situations. He and other high-level advisors are appalled that most financial representatives don't even look at a client's tax return, much less know what to look for.

Tom Gau of Oregon Pacific Financial Advisors, Inc., who coaches financial advisors on how to become substantially more productive and professional, says that part of his course deals with showing advisors what to look for in a tax return and how to read between the lines. When he asks them, "What do you look for in a tax return?" He finds that most, unfortunately, have no idea.

Periodic reviews are part of the due diligence that advisors regularly perform for their clients. Consider this: if their job is to act as a steward of your wealth, then they must be kept in the loop with respect to any changes in your situation. For example, Bill Baker of William Baker & Associates, Inc. says, "A lot of people don't realize that a significant event such as a divorce voids their will. Also, if you move a retirement account from one custodian to another, you may have to fill out a new beneficiary form. An illness may require that a power of attorney be drafted. So continual due diligence applies to all aspects of a client's financial life."

Bill's communication process helps make sure that nothing is overlooked. One of Bill's clients mentioned that he was thinking about going to Iraq. Bill asked him why, and whether he had talked to his wife about it. He said, "Oh, I didn't tell you, I'm not married any longer." As soon as Bill got off the phone, he sent the client a beneficiary update form because the former spouse was still the client's designated beneficiary.

In addition to reviews being important from a personal circumstance standpoint, they are extremely important to measure progress on planning benchmarks and to uncover changes that require action, says Bill. He introduces all of his clients to the basics of investing early on so that they have a good understanding of his investment processes. He then reviews the fundamental and technical aspects of the market and their portfolios at each subsequent meeting.

Changes in taxes and laws are another factor that advisors regularly monitor in case they need to review some aspect of the client's financial plan. For instance, Mike Piershale of Piershale Financial Group says changes in estate tax laws could affect his clients if they have not had their documents reviewed and updated within the last five years. As he looks over trusts, wills and other estate plans for new clients, he occasionally discovers important documents that are missing or outdated. Piershale states, "Over the years, as I have looked at estate plans, I have seen people invalidate a trust by signing in the wrong place, fail to re-title revocable trusts properly after the death of a spouse and work with inexperienced attorneys who excluded sections of a good estate plan that protect the family in case of the incapacity of one or both of the spouses. In some cases these oversights could have cost the heirs substantial amounts of money." As the estate laws have changed he has encouraged his clients to have all the documents reviewed to ensure compliance.

Tom Gau says that each year he finds tens of millions of dollars in errors within the documents he regularly examines for potential clients and the clients of advisors he coaches. Fortunately, he can save clients large sums of money by catching these errors. Unfortunately, he sometimes receives the information when it is already too late; he then has to suggest "next best alternatives."

Your Responsibilities

Even the best-written legal document may fail to do its job if a client fails to adhere to the provisions. It doesn't matter if it's due to forgetfulness, lack of understanding, or making certain assumptions; if you fail to follow the law, you may place yourself in financial and legal jeopardy. In the accompanying case study, an 80-year-old man had poor communication with his attorney, which almost cost him a substantial sum of money. He had excellent communication with his financial advisor, which saved him from himself. (See–*Communication*.)

Proactive and Reactive

It's obvious that competent advisors communicate with their clients, both proactively and reactively. They are proactive when they conduct their regular reviews and ask about personal and financial changes that may have occurred. They are reactive when clients tell them about changes in circumstances, or when the advisor sees changes in the economy, the market, or the law. Keeping up with everything can be a daunting task; but these advisors can do so because of the various processes that they each have in place.

Going Beyond Financial Updates

If you've had the experience of working with a high-level advisor, you'll find that they and their teams go far beyond what is expected when trying to help their clients. The case study on page 80 is a good example of how Michael Searcy made a big difference for a family because he carefully listened to his

COMMUNICATION

Yale Levey shares an interesting story about an elderly client who likes to be in control and do everything himself. He had difficulty communicating with his attorney and, as a result, fired the attorney that drafted many of his key documents.

Unfortunately, the man made a couple of major errors handling his wife's estate because of some incorrect assumptions. His errors in judgment and failure to follow the appropriate protocols would have cost his family almost $250,000 in taxes. Essentially, he just figured it was his wife's intention for him to inherit all of the money. Rather than diverting her money into a trust for his benefit, he just took the assets and transferred them into his own name.

Fortunately, the man had complete trust and open communications with Yale. When he told Yale of his wife's death, Yale offered a "second pair of eyes" to review the will before everything took effect. Fortunately, the man agreed. Yale saw what had occurred, and urged the man to find a new lawyer and reverse the error before it took effect.

As a result, the man now has a credit shelter trust with the assets properly diverted. If the man died today, the properly titled assets within the trust would save his family almost a quarter of a million dollars.

clients and then offered a creative solution. (See—*A Helping Hand*)

The point is, high-level advisors regularly go beyond the norm for their clients. When meeting with your current or potential advisors, you should ask them for examples of how they have made a difference. Listen to what they tell you. Watch their body language. Their willingness and ability to help others offers a wealth of information about their willingness and ability to help you.

Communication and Feedback Go Hand-in-Hand

Good advisors are always looking for better ways to meet your needs and are willing to listen to your suggestions for improvement. Of course, they may be unwilling or unable to make the suggested changes. If so, they should offer an explanation. Excellent advisors, on the other hand, actively seek feedback from their clients in a variety of ways. Some send out survey forms, while others ask directly or indirectly. Constructive criticism has helped many advisors improve their already impressive processes.

George Jackson conducts an annual survey to find out what he and his team are doing right and what they're doing wrong. George says, "When clients send the report back to us they let us know if they're happy or unhappy; it's helped us make some nice enhancements to the way we work with our clients. One improvement is that we're now even more proactive than we

A HELPING HAND

Michael J. Searcy asked a client what he felt was the best thing Mike had done for him over the years. The answer was, "The book thing." Mike didn't initially understand what the client was referring to, so the client had to remind him of how he made a huge difference in the lives of their two children.

Mike often suggests excellent books to his clients that he believes will help them get more out of life. Books like *Rich Dad, Poor Dad* and *The Millionaire Next Door* offer people valuable insights on life and wealth management. The couple (Mike's clients) wanted their teenage children to read the books before going to college but didn't think they could motivate them to do so. Mike discovered from the parents that the kids liked "stuff that cost money."

Mike had an idea. The next time he was at the client's house, the teens, Frank and Megan, were also there. Mike told Frank and Megan that their parents would like them to read these books. Frank responded, "Yeah, yeah," and Megan said she was too busy. Mike told them that if they would read the book, write up a report on it, and sit down and talk with their parents about the book's relevance to their lives, each would get a $100 bill. He held the bills up for them to see.

Both Frank and Megan graduated college and are becoming successful in their respective fields. Their parents said that getting them to read a few insightful books, including the two mentioned, opened their eyes to a wider understanding of finances and the world. The clients/parents said it was the cheapest investment they ever made, and they credited Mike with helping to steer Frank and Megan onto the right track.

Mike says that he and his team have a "servant's heart." According to Mike, "If you're there to serve the needs of your clients, without any bias or objective, without trying to sell them something, without any conflicts, and all you're trying to do is take care of them, then it [the advisory business] will work."

were before."

Other advisors offer similar comments and made improvement such as:

- Improved the "readability" of reports
- Reduced the volume of paper for certain clients and increased it for others, developed additional educational seminars, met with entire families privately to discuss legacy issues
- Created special reports or white papers to address different investment, tax, and legal issues

Investor Responsibilities

Needless to say, advisors can only do so much or be so proactive. It is incumbent upon you to communicate your needs to your advisor and, especially, inform him or her of any changes in your circumstances.

While each of the advisors interviewed here has a system in place to maintain regular contact with clients, there may be greater urgency to talk if there is a sudden health issue, a death in the family, some unexpected loss, etc. Below are a few of the events that should trigger a call to your advisor. Each represents an event that may require the modification of some part of your financial strategy.

Such situations include:

- Birth of a child
- Change in investment objectives
- Divorce, separation
- Death of a spouse
- Unexpected liabilities
- Taking over responsibility for a parent
- Change in the will
- Major illness
- Terminated from employment
- Receive stock bonus
- Receive inheritance
- Purchase or liquidate a major asset
- Lawsuit (you or any member of your family)
- Sale or purchase of house

Brian Puckett of Brian Puckett Retirement Advisors says he reviews his clients' objectives quarterly. "We see every client face-to-face for a quarterly review. Once they become comfortable with us, some of those reviews can be done over the phone."

"I am always asking, tell me what's gong on in your life? Had any changes? Get married? Divorced? Any new kids? I really love developing close relationships with my clients. Wealth management is a very personal business. So I talk to my clients frequently not only about money, but also about their lives... their kids, grandkids, what they are excited about and what they are worried about," he says.

Brian also asks other questions, such as: "How's your health?" "Are there any health issues in the family that may require either your time or your money to be allocated to it?" "What's worrying you?" "What is keeping you awake at night these days?"

"We also have a formal, not stuffy, annual meeting where we review their plan and discuss what has happened during the past year," he says. Of course, if anything unexpected has developed, his team will examine it in detail. They want to make sure that their clients are headed in the right direction.

Brian will also review all the investment parameters and returns to make sure that he and his clients are "on the same page." For example, his clients can expect to hear something like: "Here's the range of returns that we will likely get from this mixture of investments. Is this still the goal of our work together? If not, what adjustments should be made?"

Sometimes adjustments are considered and examined in light of all other aspects of the plan. Nothing is done in a vacuum because a change in one part a person's financial life can impact something quite unrelated. We must keep in mind that when you pick up one end of a stick, you pick up the other end of the stick too. Let us be conscious of the consequences of all our actions. That way we can be deliberate and accurate.

Miscommunications, Mistakes, and Misalignments

"I know you understand what you think I said, but I'm not so sure that what you heard is what I meant."

This saying is written in jest, but the reality is, miscommunication can prove disastrous in financial situations. Miscommunications are not always easy to identify, but there are a number of signs you and your advisor can be on the lookout for, as well as a number of useful remedies.

This section discusses some "red flags" that can signal trouble or incompatibility between you and an advisor.

Red Flags from the Investor's Perspective

Caution: Small problems that occur early on could be an indication of bigger problems later. Small problems made by an advisor can include: incorrectly spelling your name and not taking the time to fix it, not returning a telephone call or e-mail request within a reasonable time, not sending out materials on a timely basis, and not keeping good notes.

Ask yourself these questions:

- Are they following through on things they said they were going to do

—even simple things like mailing paperwork to you? They should "do what they say, say what they do."

- Are they giving you a straightforward, fair answer, or do they beat around the bush?
- Do they communicate with you frequently? If you are not talking to your advisor or your advisor's staff member at least once a quarter, it could be a problem.
- Have the ground rules and processes they laid out been followed? For example, at the first meeting did the advisor explain what he or she does and the management process that he or she uses?
- Do they really listen to you and verify their understanding?
- Do they put agreements in writing?
- Do they use jargon and talk above your head?
- Do they focus only on transactions?
- Are the advisor's team members responsive to your needs?
- Do they seem to hide things from you either directly or by being evasive?

Often, these things are indications of simple mistakes that can be quickly fixed. But if the problem is not resolved after one or two attempts to fix it, then you and your advisor are not communicating effectively with each other. If it isn't resolved, you need to consider whether or not to continue the relationship.

Perhaps the biggest red flag is when an advisor doesn't attempt to periodically update your financial profile. After all, if your needs have shifted for whatever reason, then adaptations must be made to your plan.

Red Flags From the Advisor's Perspective

Red flags go both ways. Advisors must be sensitive to potential changes in client attitude, commitment, and responses. Advisors generally noted the following as cause for concern:

- Failing to return phone calls
- Frequent changes of investment objectives
- Failing to provide complete and accurate information
- Wishing to trade in the market (if that was not part of the original plan)
- Regular references to what other representatives are saying/doing
- Arguing, challenging recommendations as opposed to asking
- Asking for reduced fees
- Expecting inappropriate levels of service
- Not listening to the advisor's advice
- Being unpleasant or rude team members

If you or your advisor feels that there is a "misalignment" of purposes, then you both need to assess what is going on and communicate with each other. Most of the time the issue or concern is simple and can be quickly resolved. Allowing any type of dissatisfaction to fester does a disservice to everyone.

Parting Ways

In the vast majority of situations advisors and clients are able to resolve their differences. Again, such differences are usually the result of miscommunication or poor assumptions. It is not uncommon for an advisor and client to part ways. However, it does occur, and there are circumstances when there is no longer a good "fit" between the two parties. Here are short stories from three of our advisors who discuss why certain relationships weren't a good fit for them.

Example #1: Cella Quinn describes a situation where she had a client who was a confirmed stock trader and would call Cella saying, "I just saw this story on CNN about XYZ company. Would you look into it?" However, Cella found that it was taking too much time out of her schedule to do a thorough analysis. Far better, she felt, to spend her time following a select group of funds rather than trying to learn a little about thousands of individual companies. Says Cella, This client was not a good fit. If I have a client who doesn't like funds, it is in their best interest to go elsewhere."

"It was like the Gretna High School (NE) football team playing the University of Nebraska Cornhuskers," she says. This client was not a good fit. If I have a client who doesn't like funds, it is in their best interest to go elsewhere.

Example #2: Bill Baker says, "I've suggested on several occasions that I do not think we are a match and that the client probably ought to look elsewhere for someone who better aligns with their expectations." He adds, "Greed-driven and fear-driven investors are usually one and the same person. They ride the emotional roller coaster and are sometimes good contra-indicators to the market. They want to be 15 percent CD investors–all upside and no toleration for downside. Not good client material for us."

Example #3: Mike Piershale tells about a retired client who would not share all the necessary information Mike needed in order to give him proper advice. When something would go wrong, however, this client held Mike responsible. "This was a person who became a client a number of years ago, before we transitioned into fee-based financial planning. Frankly, if he would not share needed information today he would not have become a client," he says.

This client said he had found an insurance-backed investment that guaranteed an 18 percent yield where the principal would never fluctuate. Mike asked to see the documentation on this "super investment," which the client failed to produce. Mike felt at that point that this relationship had reached its end. The client never followed his advice, did not give Mike any personal financial information, and always talked about how great his other investments were doing without ever letting Mike see the statements.

Mike politely disengaged himself from that client.

Clear Communication is an Art and Science

While there are many ways to communicate ideas that have been described here, helping people to comprehend complex topics is probably the most difficult.

An advisor can tell a client that a certain investment is risky, but it is much more powerful to paint a mental picture of what risk entails so that clients have a true appreciation, not just an intellectual appreciation, of risk. Usually advisors have preferred analogies, metaphors, stories, and examples that make certain complex topics simple to understand – often giving an "ah-hah!" experience – especially for those investors who are not advanced students of investing.

Advisor Cella Quinn uses an analogy with her clients to help them better understand the differences between the various investment products: "Some growth mutual funds are like driving about 75 miles per hour down a six-lane highway," she says.. "If you invest in a growth and income fund, you're driving around 65 mph. And with other types of funds you may be moving at 45 or 50 mph. They'll all eventually get to the same place, but some will take more risk in getting there and some will take longer." She continues, "The problem is that people see the other lanes moving faster and want to jump into a faster lane, but by the time they switch into that lane, it slows down. So it's better to have a car in more than one lane."

This analogy is a perfect way to explain how some investors are influenced by the faster traffic during a bull market. They want to switch, but don't consider that the market is erratic. What may be the ideal investment today, may be the worst investment next year, and vice versa. It also addresses how your advisor helps you stay focused on your goals and objectives.

In Conclusion

There are many ways advisors can communicate with you during each phase of the relationship. None is intrinsically better than another. What matters is that you understand each other and make an effort to keep each other informed of changes in circumstances.

◆◆◆

Baker on Integrity

"Integrity is a key ingredient to building lasting and meaningful relationships in business and all of life. Components of integrity are honesty, trustworthiness, straight talk and intent. The example of integrity in day-to-day actions and interactions is set and flows from the leadership and through the organization outward.

Integrity combined with wisdom and competence is a winning combination for great achievement. What we say is important, saying what we say clearly and with respect and consideration for others is important, knowing how to listen well is important, and carrying through on what we say and what we promise is important.

To build a culture of integrity requires that each of us: set the example of ethical behavior, deliver more than what we promise, encourage openness and understand when mistakes are made –admit, resolve, learn and go on, deal with observed breaches of integrity quickly, and do a personal integrity check every morning in front of the mirror. Yes it does require being a student of integrity and working at it every day.

At the end, much of our legacy is the model of service and integrity that we, through our example, set forth for those who follow."

William Baker, Principal/Founder
William Baker & Associates, Inc.

Chapter 10

EVALUATE, EXECUTE, RE-EVALUATE

PROCESS: Evaluate
- To appraise or determine the value of.

PROCESS: Execute
- To do or carry out fully.
- To put in force.

Implementing a financial plan and checking the results are important components of the PROCESS.

Evaluation of the Initial Plan

Unless you are a highly trained advisor yourself, it would be difficult to fully evaluate a proposed plan of action; after all, you hired your advisor to create something outside your personal area of expertise. Yet, you should feel satisfied with the plan based on how your advisor understands your needs, is able to put them into writing, and describes the "logic" of the plan or strategy.

The advisor will put the plan in writing to create a document that you can refer to in the future. This document, referred to by names such as a financial plan, Investment Policy Statement (IPS), a plan of action, or an investment plan, will be the basis of ongoing evaluations. The name often depends upon the purpose of the document, your personal needs and preferences, its complexity, and the advisor's preferred system. They all have in common the following:

- A statement of your goals and objectives
- A series of steps that are recommended
- Benchmarks to measure effectiveness

Depending upon the complexity of the plan, most advisors will have it internally reviewed by another team member. This is part of their review process to make sure that all bases are covered. After all, we're all human and a second set of eyes may notice a deficiency. The Hutchinson/Ifrah Financial Services team, for example, has a dozen financial planners on staff. Within their system every financial plan created is reviewed and approved by a second financial planner with a CFP designation who did not participate in the original work. As Eric Hutchinson says, "Our system has numerous checks and balances to make sure the client is always getting CFP-level advice." His team also consists of people with other designations that can participate in the review process.

Michael Searcy concurs, and adds that the document is a tool for ensuring that nothing is overlooked with clients. Also, as part of his system or process, every client gets assigned a team of two people – their primary advisor and a financial planning associate. With two people working with each client, there are two sets of eyes watching over the various components related to their planning.

Everything is documented in writing so that the team always has a "track" to follow. This helps Searcy Financial Services and the client see where they started, what has occurred along the way, where everything stands currently, and what the plan is for the future. As Mike says, "It's harder for things to slip through the cracks when it is in writing." Additionally, he says, project management software is used to monitor pending activities, to assign projects, and to see what tasks have already been completed or resolved for the client. This also provides them with a way to document everything electronically so that anyone in the firm can easily see what's going on with a particular client and can service that client's needs more efficiently if the primary planner or financial planning associate is out of the office.

Unfortunately, many major financial firms will not allow their sales representatives to produce such a document for you. How can anyone help you realize your dreams if they don't know what they are and if they haven't taken the time to write them into a customized, objective plan? How can they even be expected to remember the details for each of their potentially hundreds of clients?

With regard to the need for a written plan, consider the following questions:

- What would happen if the advisor were to die or leave the business?

Without written documentation the new advisor or representative would have to start from scratch.

- What would happen if you died or became incapacitated? Not knowing the plan of action could be harmful to your estate or long-term plans.
- What if someone was to recommend another investment and you didn't have the services of the original advisor? You'd have no real way of evaluating how the investment would fit into the overall equation.
- Do you have total recall? Probably not. Being human, we only remember a small percentage of what we hear, especially as time passes.
- What if there is a misunderstanding regarding services that are to be rendered? A written plan can come to the rescue.
- What happens if your expectations are unconsciously modified – for better or worse – by market actions? The written plan has benchmarks that you can refer to.

Cella Quinn believes the information in most financial plans is 95 percent boilerplate. Only five percent specifically applies to the investor who paid for the plan. Thus, she finds very few are actually read and even fewer are followed because most clients don't read more than a few pages. She questions clients about plans prepared by another financial planner and finds that very few can answer her questions. Of course, a few people have read and memorized their plans, but they are extremely rare. Cella comments, "Most people pay a lot of money for a financial plan and then never look at it again. Kind of like an exercise program."

Cella's portfolio reviews are always customized for each client. Reviews are done whenever her evaluation process triggers them or at least yearly, to make certain the investments and their current and expected performances are in line with a client's goals and objectives. People need to know what they paid for each investment and its current worth. How else can they track whether their net worth is increasing or not?

Highlighting the need for a written, customized plan, Bill Baker of William Baker & Associates, Inc. says, "We look at the financial plan as a helpful roadmap. It can be used as a benchmarking tool and should be periodically reviewed and updated as the client's situation changes. Things happen. People may inherit money, they may have to deplete their nest egg for some emergency, they may change occupations; and so, a financial plan is very useful to measure progress and to adapt to changing circumstances."

"A plan does not have to be very elaborate. For a young person it may be just a single page showing annual investments necessary to build a retirement nest egg, coverage of risk-management issues (insurances), powers of attorney, a will, and a living will. It should be written down to ensure that all relevant issues are dealt with."

Bill further explains that an Investment Policy Statement (IPS) is a document that must be produced for certain legal entities, such as foundations and pension plans, and can be produced for others depending on their needs. He says an IPS is a useful tool for the advisor and the client; it helps ensure they are on the same wavelength with regard to the investment game plan – asset allocation approach, expected returns over time, risk tolerance, risk management, liquidity and cash flow needs, tax issues, investment constraints, and so forth.

Michael Searcy concurs, and adds that the document is a tool for ensuring that nothing is overlooked. Everything is documented in writing so that the team always has a "track" to follow. This helps Searcy Financial Services and the client see where they started, what has occurred along the way, where everything stands currently, and what the plan is for the future. As Michael says, "It's harder for things to slip through the cracks when it is in writing." Additionally, he says, project management software is used to monitor pending activities, to assign projects, and to see what tasks have already been completed or resolved for the client. This also provides them with a way to document everything electronically so that anyone in the firm can easily see what's going on with a particular client and can service that client's needs more efficiently if the primary planner or financial planning associate is out of the office.

High-level advisors spend a lot of time creating customized plans for you, as an individual. They take into account your unique needs, goals, and desires.

Beware of computer-generated financial plans created by a sales representative. These plans involve having you check some boxes; the answers are used to categorize you as a pre-set "type" of investor. The computer then spits out a plan of action for you to follow over your lifetime. These are plans for the "generic" client; however, there is no such thing as a generic client.

Next Step – Execution

"Sometimes, ya just gotta do it."

Clients, in most cases, can easily see the logic of the advisor's plan of action and are willing to immediately implement the suggestions. However, some clients avoid executing the plan of action for a host of reasons, including:

- ***Fear of change.*** Many adults are "change-phobic." The thought of changing jobs, relationships, residences, etc., is extremely disquieting to them. A knot forms in the pit of their stomachs, and they do nothing. But not making a decision is, in fact, making a decision -- albeit a poor one.

- ***Procrastination.*** "I'll do it tomorrow," they say, and tomorrow never comes. It's easy to postpone things; but days turn into weeks, weeks into months, and months into years. The next thing you know, nothing has been done and it's too late.
- ***Paralysis by analysis.*** People who go to extremes exploring and evaluating different alternatives often end up doing nothing. This "need to know it all" syndrome paralyzes the decision-making process.
- ***"I'm too busy."*** Often people are too busy to do what is necessary to make dramatic changes in their lives. We all run the risk of being too busy and allowing life to pass us by. If someone is too busy, perhaps he or she should delegate some of the tasks to competent people. If they delegate the crucial job of financial planning to an expert, they can spend more time enjoying life.
- ***"Need to talk it over" or "Let me think about it" syndromes.*** Occasionally, these responses are appropriate. The problem occurs when people get mixed messages by talking to too many people, experts or otherwise. If an investor needs to "think about it," it usually implies one or more issues or questions have not been discussed. In this case, the investor needs to go to his or her advisor for an answer and then make a decision.

Advisors want you to feel comfortable with your decision and know that you are committed to the plan, so they don't mind you talking it over – with a spouse or another professional, for example. Whereas, sales representatives often want you to immediately sign on the dotted line. They will push you to make a quick decision.

- ***Mistrust.*** Trust is usually developed after the investor has met with an advisor, checked his or her credentials and references, and become familiar with the advisor's process. If this doesn't happen or there is a breakdown along the way, mistrust occurs.
- ***Fear of failure.*** Fear takes many forms: fear of making a mistake; fear that the market might drop; or fear that you may need more money. You should have an equal or greater fear of doing nothing.
- ***Greed.*** This manifests itself through the belief that the market is about to go up or will continue to rise and the desire to capture additional profits rather than take the more appropriate courses of action, such as taking profits and reinvesting the proceeds into more conservative investments. Greed causes more portfolio disasters than almost any other factor.
- ***"Tail wagging the dog" syndrome.*** Investors who won't take a profit because they'll have to pay taxes on huge capital gains. While

understandable, there are a number of different strategies that can be employed.

Re-Evaluate the Results

Once the financial plan has been operating for a while, previously established measurable goals can be objectively evaluated. Is your plan on track? What is the specific performance of your portfolio? How is it doing relative to certain benchmarks? You and the advisor should be evaluating the portfolio based on whether it is behaving within the parameters established within your financial plan.

It is also important to periodically re-evaluate your goals and objectives, as described in the previous chapter on communications. People's lives do not remain static. Circumstances, attitudes, beliefs, needs and goals change. What was true today or 10 years ago may not be true 10 years from now. Therefore, when you re-evaluate performance, do so against both what you originally wanted and then against what you may want. Remember that the advisor can make mid-course corrections in the plan.

Nothing is Perfect

Despite a thorough selection process, there will be times when the results of a particular investment or money manager are less than expected. This, in and of itself, is not necessarily bad because only one investment or one manager out of many is affected. The advisor is monitoring the overall portfolio and taking into account that one investment or manager may be doing unexpectedly better for the same reason another one is doing worse.

Monitoring the Professional Money Manager

How do advisors monitor portfolio performance? They have numerous sophisticated tools to help them determine where and how managers add value. They'll usually monitor performance over a full market cycle because they realize that there is no "best" approach to the market. A series of overlapping, yet non-simultaneous, cycles actually drive the investments markets based upon numerous domestic and international economic factors.

The construction of an efficient portfolio requires the selection of different approaches or styles of investing. As one style of investing comes into favor, another may be falling out of favor, and still another may be static. It's all built into the equation to get you the expected rate of return. It's important for money managers to stay with their discipline or style even when it is out of favor because if they speculate (diverge or drift from their style) to boost their results, they can skew the results and leave the overall portfolio in a more speculative position than it should be.

Different Strokes for Different Folks

While some individual advisors make stock and/or bond decisions on their own, others rely on a partner or member of an internal team. Most employ the services of professional money managers who specialize in the day-to-day and month-to-month movements of the stock market.

For instance, Bill Baker and his team have a process for selecting and monitoring stocks that he calls a security watch list system based on a very disciplined research process with automated alert systems. They also have a statement-tracking tool that tracks bottom-line values from year-end to year-end and month-to-month. This system prompts them to contact a client if significant changes in statement value occur. Additionally, he and his team use other watch-list and transaction execution tools. See case study "Tools of the Trade."

Cella Quinn prefers to "buy the brains" of some of the best money managers in the world by using a carefully selected group of mutual funds that have a history of maintaining their style disciplines throughout a market cycle (as described in Chapter 9). She conducts a formal review of the entire portfolio compared to client objectives at least once a year.

She's alert to factors such as a change in portfolio managers or a manager underperforming his or her benchmark. At that point she'll

TOOLS OF THE TRADE

Bill Baker, William Baker & Associates, uses a sophisticated method for asset allocation, security selection, and risk management based on fundamental and technical analysis.

To put it in simple language he uses an analogy rephrased from his technical research provider, Dorsey Wright & Associates, Inc. Bill says "If I had to boil investment management down to three things it would be these. Using a sport's analogy, first I would want to know which team to have on the field—offensive or defensive. Offensive team suggests more market exposure, defensive team suggests less. Second I would want to know what my field position was (i.e. high level of market and sector risk or low level of market and sector risk) and third I would want to have a very good idea of who my strongest players were for the situation and put them into play. (i.e. I want those securities in play with the best fundamental and relative strength compared to the market and their peer group)

He says to stack the odds in your client's favor requires a proven methodology, excellence in research, continual due diligence, and effective execution. "It requires having the research, technology, and the experience to ferret out opportunity and to quickly manage risk when risk goes against you. We corroborate fundamental research with technical (or capital markets supply and demand) research. Just using one body of research would in our judgment be like working with an incomplete set of tools—not good for the client."

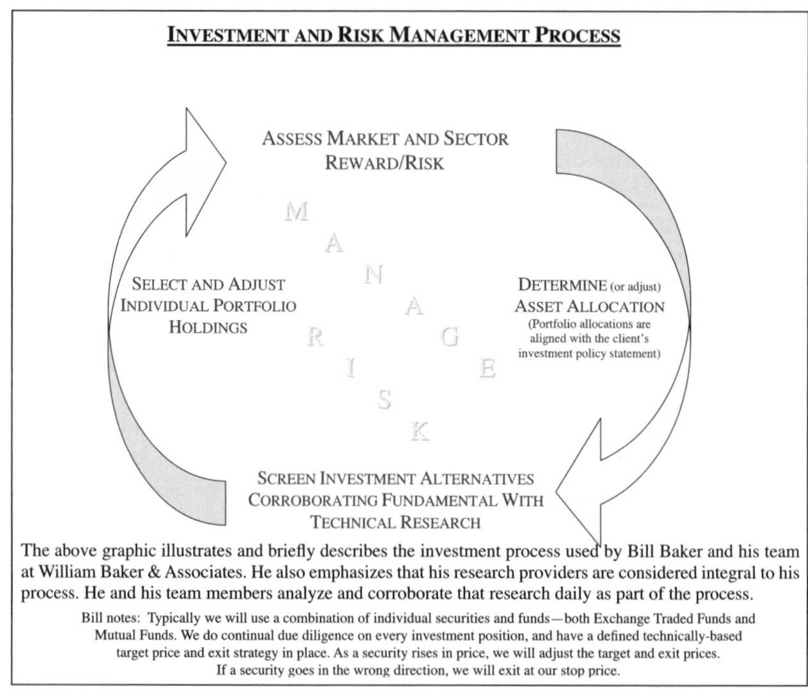

The above graphic illustrates and briefly describes the investment process used by Bill Baker and his team at William Baker & Associates. He also emphasizes that his research providers are considered integral to his process. He and his team members analyze and corroborate that research daily as part of the process.

Bill notes: Typically we will use a combination of individual securities and funds—both Exchange Traded Funds and Mutual Funds. We do continual due diligence on every investment position, and have a defined technically-based target price and exit strategy in place. As a security rises in price, we will adjust the target and exit prices. If a security goes in the wrong direction, we will exit at our stop price.

find out why and, if necessary, alert her clients to what is happening and recommend a course of action.

Reasonable Versus Unreasonable Expectations

Despite all of the historical evidence and logic to the contrary, many investors still lose their perspective because of unreasonable, unattainable expectations. Many of the advisors quoted in this book reference the bull market of the 1990s as a time when many investors formed unrealistic expectations. Throughout history, in the vast majority of bull-market cycles there comes a point at which an investor's enthusiasm and exuberance overshadows logic and discipline. They think: "Everybody's making money," "There's no where to go but up!" "Today's highs are tomorrow's lows!" and, "This is a new economy, the old rules don't apply." Somewhere near the market peak, over-enthusiasm and unrealistic expectations reach their highest pitch. At this point (and its polar opposite) many investors want to shift gears by using an investment strategy that will make fast, easy money. But it doesn't work that way.

Craig Pluta and Chris Doughty of the ReAct! Group say that during the period mentioned above, many of their competitors were promising people the ability to withdraw a conservative 10 percent annually on their portfolio because "things had changed" and 10 percent was "conservative." Craig and Chris knew differently. Based upon historical standards and their realization that the high growth rates of the 1990s were an anomaly, they advised clients to be truly conservative. In hindsight, those other competitors (sales representatives) may have received more commissions by convincing people to their way of thinking, but later lost most, if not all, of those clients because of their lack of appreciation for market conditions and its consequences.

Craig and Chris comment that the 1990s bull market created a "decision point" in their careers: Should they follow the group-think (like most other advisors) or should they do what they knew was right and protect their clients, even though it was both less profitable to them and somewhat unpopular with their clients? They chose to maintain their personal and professional integrity. They refused to offer excessive rates of projected growth or withdrawal rates. In doing so, they still retained most of their clients. As Chris says, "we decided to take the path less traveled, and it has made all difference for us and our clients."

Many advisors say that if they can help clients avoid just one big mistake then they have provided significant value. Without a doubt, Craig Pluta and Chris Doughty helped their clients avoid a huge mistake that spelled financial disaster for millions of other investors.

Managing Expectations

One of an advisor's most difficult jobs is managing investor expectations––and getting them to continue to follow the plan. Expectations, reasonable or unreasonable, become an unconscious part of the evaluation and re-evaluation process. Advisors strive to add logic and objectivity to the evaluation process through the use of charts, historical correlations, reasonable projections, etc. – all with the hope of keeping their clients on the course that was originally set.

In Conclusion

A multifaceted evaluation process helps you evaluate the logic of an investment or financial plan, helps an advisor evaluate money managers and the performance of the portfolio, and helps you conduct a self-evaluation to ensure you don't get caught up in the emotions of the market. Once you've seen the logic of the plan devised by your advisor, you owe it to yourself, your family, and your legacy to implement it.

◆◆◆

Gau on Integrity

"Integrity is just like Karma to me. This means to always do the right thing. This includes placing the interest of the client first and always giving objective advice, regardless of compensation. In order for this to happen, trust is a key ingredient. We only gain this trust by acting with integrity at all times with our clients."

Thomas B. Gau, CPA, CFP®, CRIA
Principal
Oregon Pacific Financial Advisors, Inc.

Chapter 11

SYSTEMS, SYSTEMS, EVERYWHERE:

But Are They Right For You?

PROCESS: Systems

- Assemblage of objects arranged after some distinct method.
- Whole scheme of created things regarded as forming one complete whole.
- Organization.
- Set of doctrines or principles.

So far, this book has explored various attributes that contribute to the individualized system each advisor employs. This chapter will delve more deeply into the actual systems these advisors have in place, and then concentrate on whether or not your personality and character attributes are a good match for these types of advisory teams, or whether you're better off doing it yourself or using a financial sales representative.

You Are Part of the System

When you work with a high-level advisor and advisory team, you become an integral part of their system. It is your needs and aspirations that trigger the various mechanisms within their process. If there is a change in your circumstances, the system ensures that the appropriate people are contacted, the right questions asked, and the correct adaptations made to your plan and investments. For example, if changes in the law occur, the system ensures that those clients being affected are notified, and that the appropriate adaptations occur in each individual's financial plan.

Advisory Systems That Work for You

When you engage the services of a high-level financial advisor, you engage more than his or her knowledge, experience, dedication, and concern. You also engage an entire system of people, technology, resources and relationships that ensure the financial planning or investment process will occur seamlessly each and every time. At least, that's the way the process is intended to work. In reality, does every single sub-system and procedure work perfectly each and every time? Of course not. But in many cases, because these high-level advisors have built the operating systems themselves, fine-tuned them over time, and are dedicated to constantly making everything work better, they have the knowledge to fix and improve the system themselves.

The components of the operating system take many forms – technology, people, processes – many of which are reviewed in this book and include:

- Performance evaluation systems are used so advisors can monitor the performance of money managers throughout the industry.
- Client-contact systems are in place to ensure that each client is contacted and updates occur on a regularly scheduled basis. (High-level advisors don't just call to sell you something.)
- Team systems are in place to ensure that a coordinated effort is made on your behalf. Cross training of personnel is just one example.
- Professional continuing education is pursued by advisors and many of the team members to upgrade their skills and knowledge.
- A network of other professionals is in place to assist advisors when necessary.
- The investment process has been designed and implemented; it is upgraded on a regular basis.
- Internal teams are in place, and each member provides a key component of your overall financial advisory needs.
- Client education is provided when needed, and sometimes offered in a seminar or workshop setting.

The chart on the next page illustrates a system an advisor may have in place for servicing clients. Each advisor has spent countless hours developing similar systems, that have proven to be effective over the years and are constantly being refined. Some of the improvements come from feedback provided by clients – constructive criticism, if you will. Other improvements come from experiencing the various market highs and lows, attending various industry conferences, interactions with peers and professionals from other disciplines, and a lot of trial and error. Implementing constant improvements is one way these high-level advisors differentiate themselves from traditional advisors.

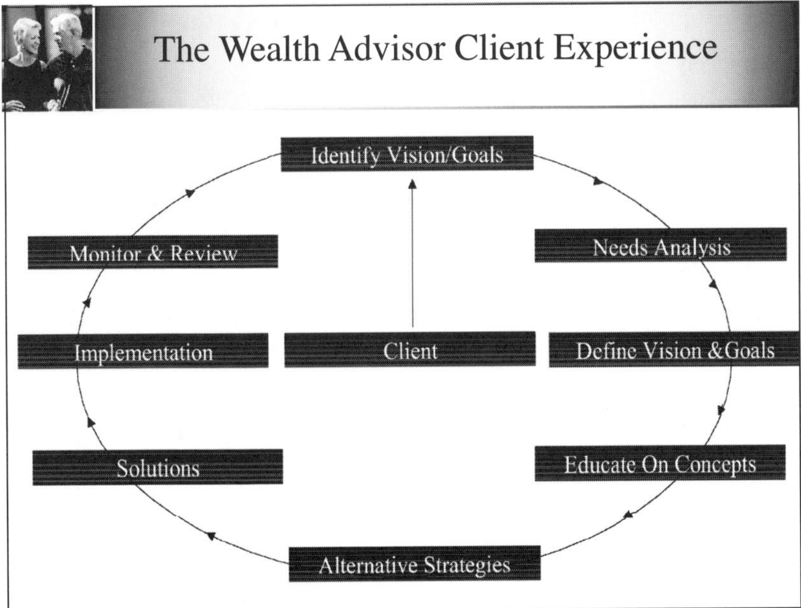

Are These Systems Right for *You*?

Listed on pages 100-101 are some of the characteristics and attitudes the advisors in this book believe describe an ideal client. This list is not presented in any particular order, nor is there 100 percent consensus. Nevertheless, it should provide you with a good idea of the type of client high-level advisors prefer most.

Ultimately, the question you have to answer is: *"Do I want to join the system of care, with all of its checks and balances, offered by a high-level advisor? Or, do I want to do it all myself?"*

Michael Searcy of Searcy Financial Services elegantly sums up the different types of investors as he describes four groups of people and how they handle their personal investments.

- "The first group are those who do it themselves. They enjoy it, they're good at it, and they are willing to spend the time doing it. Such people don't generally make great clients for advisors because they're doing their own thing.
- The second group are those who do it themselves and may even enjoy it, but they're not really good at it. Such people make good clients because we can really help them.
- Then there are those who probably could do it themselves, but realize that it would not be the best use of their time, talents and resources. They'd rather be spending their precious time doing something they really enjoy. These people make great clients for us because they un-

TRAITS AN ADVISOR LOOKS FOR IN A CLIENT

Yale Levey:

"Someone who is open-minded and thinks outside the box. We want to work with clients who are coachable (teachable) and are open to our suggestions and recommendations. Someone who can articulate his or her expectations and wants a plan created by design, rather than just letting things happen by default. People who have a love for life, the people in their lives, and the causes they support."

Cella Quinn:

"I like people who are intellectually bright and driven to creating wealth.I left home at the age of 16 with $44 in my pocket. I know how to build wealth and want clients who are willing to let me help them do the same."

George Jackson:

"People hire me because they want a life. They want me to manage the complexities of taxes, investments, and estate planning. They are usually looking for a one-stop shop."

Michael Searcy:

"Rather than [work with] someone who is independent and picks my brain for ideas to implement themselves so they can save a couple of bucks, I prefer to work with people who are interdependent. They recognize that no one knows it all and that it's important to work in a collaborative fashion by coordinating with a variety of professionals, who are all working together to achieve the best results."

Mike Piershale:

"We're not looking for 'do-it-yourselfers.' We're looking for people who recognize that we're going to know more about this business than they do. While we do have some do-it-yourselfers, it's because they were tired of doing everything themselves or because they had spouses that lacked their financial sophistication and they wanted to be sure those spouses were taken care of in case of death or incapacity."

Craig Pluta and Chris Doughty:

"We want clients who are willing to open up and not hold anything back. It's no different than holding back information from a doctor, who will not be able to make a proper diagnosis. There should be mutual respect and a genuine rapport so that they are willing to listen to the advisor with an open mind."

Tom Gau:

"Our ideal clients are those who want us to be their financial quarterback, who realize they can't do it themselves, and who are willing to delegate."

Eric Hutchinson:

"My ideal clients either don't want to do this work themselves, or they don't feel that they can. They are willing to consider delegating responsibility to a trained, trusted advisor. "

William Baker:

"The best-suited clients for our approach are individuals who are of high integrity, and responsible people who are successful in their own right. We look for clients who are realistic in their expectations, who have a conservative bent and who, after being educated on our investment approach, are comfortable with a risk-managed, proactive investment methodology. We prefer clients who want to go forward with a financial planning roadmap that can benchmark progress and be easily updated as their situation changes."

Brian Puckett:

"Our clients want to be good stewards of their wealth. However, like all people, they have important things they care about other than money. This allows us to step in and add value by making sure that everything is really working the way it should be while the clients pursue the things they want to spend their time on.

Mark Little:

"My clients are really smart. They could do what I do if they put their minds to it. They might have to go back to school or take courses, but they could do it. They don't hire me because I'm smarter, but because of all of the other things in life that are more important to them than money, like relationships, health, and spiritual. Managing money is the only thing on the list that can be delegated, so by working with me they can do all of the other things that are more important."

derstand what's going on; we continue to educate them, we continue to be a resource for them, and we are basically facilitating all types of things for them."

- The final group are those who don't do it themselves and don't want to do it themselves; and they need help. So from our perspective, the only time that someone should go it alone is if he or she falls into that first category. The other three categories would be people who would be better served if they hired a confident and trustworthy advisor to help them."

[Author's Note: Even the first category of clients, those who like to do it themselves, may benefit from a relationship with a high-level wealth management team that can offer a second opinion and will undoubtedly have access to a variety of professional resources.]

In determining client suitability for a high-level advisor, Tom Gau of Oregon Pacific Financial Advisors asks a series of questions. He begins by asking his primary client if his or her spouse will be able to handle their financial affairs. Then he tells them, "If you are ever going to do something really well, there are three questions you need to consider:

1) Do you have the appropriate education? When asked if they have an in-depth financial education, most people answer 'no.' 2) Do you have the time? What about your spouse? One client is the principal of a school,

and Tom asked her if she really had the time to devote to investing. Upon reflection, she said 'no.' 3) Do you have the desire? Would you rather be managing your money, or golfing, or playing with your grandchildren, or whatever else you like to do?"

Tom's point is that unless you have the right answer to all three questions, there will come a time when you say "oops" because something was overlooked. Hopefully, it won't be a mistake that costs a lot of money.

What Advisors Think Clients (You) Really Want

Each of the advisors in this book wants to make a difference in the lives of their clients – whether it's to help them make better investments, create a financial plan that will help them accomplish their objectives, help them attain what they want from life, or simply to refer them to someone who can better assist them. These advisors are people who truly care. They are willing to take on the responsibility for helping clients identify, define and achieve their personal goals, and they believe that they are the right people for the job.

These advisors strive to provide what their clients want from them. The advisors attract, usually through referrals, like-minded clients who mesh with their personalities and approaches to doing business. The client and advisor agree to work with each other after determining that there is an appropriate match of personality, needs, capabilities, size of accounts, and other important factors. But, of course, that is merely the beginning of the relationship.

Whether the advisor *really* cares and is willing to take responsibility for recommendations still remains to be seen.

Caring is demonstrated in many ways. Caring means being there during emergencies, going beyond the norm by being helpful, providing exemplary service, being proactive, and more.

Willingness to take responsibility can also be proven in a number of ways. These advisors put things in writing – a hallmark of high-level advisors – and hold themselves and their clients accountable for the accomplishment of various goals and objectives. If something doesn't occur the way they anticipated, they don't hide behind myriad excuses, such as: "I didn't know/realize/think/understand ..." "The market went down," "The economy took a dive," etc. When they don't know something, they seek expert help from their established network of professionals, they make contingency plans for various market and economic events, and they think things through.

This all leads up to a discussion on fiduciary responsibility.

Fiduciary Responsibility and Standards of Care

According to *Barron's Dictionary of Finance and Investment Terms*, a fiduciary is "a person, company, or association holding assets in trust for a beneficiary. The fiduciary is charged with the responsibility of investing the money wisely for the beneficiary's benefit."

You should expect your advisor to think of himself or herself as a steward of your money or as a fiduciary. Whether you are responsible for your own money or that of a company, pick an advisor who has a strong sense of responsibility for your welfare.

The definition of fiduciary and the laws of fiduciary responsibility vary from state to state, but the consensus of the advisors in this book is that, regardless of the legal definition, if a person or institution relies upon you for advice, then you are a fiduciary and you have a moral, ethical, and, perhaps, legal responsibility to that person. Additionally, while some financial firms make the legal argument that providing advice to clients is only incidental to providing trade execution, most industry professionals believe that financial advisors should hold themselves to a higher standard. Whether an advisor holds the title of Investment Advisor, Registered Investment Advisor, Account Executive, Financial Advisor, Financial Consultant or Investment Planner, the name implies that he or she has a certain level of knowledge that makes him or her capable of helping investors select appropriate financial products or strategies. While the client makes the final investment decision, it is often strongly influenced by, or totally dependent on, the recommendation(s) made by the advisor.

Here are some of the comments made by advisors regarding being a fiduciary.

Brian Puckett of Brian Puckett Retirement Advisors says, "The difference between the traditional broker and what we do is that we gladly accept the responsibility of being a steward and a fiduciary of any assets that are entrusted to us for an individual and that individual's family."

Eric Hutchinson of Hutchinson/Ifrah Financial Services adds an important point about the difference between traditional representatives who are employed by some financial firms and advisors who would be considered more independent. "Within the traditional financial services environment, the fiduciary responsibility is more to the [employing] company than it is to the client; while in the registered investment advisory [independent] environment, the responsibility is to the client first. That's a very subtle but significant distinction."

The best way to precisely define the fiduciary responsibility of an advisor would be to make it a law. At the time of writing, the Securities & Exchange Commission (SEC) is considering this issue. Until then, you must rely on an advisor exercising moral responsibility and personal ethics.

Until the issue is resolved and uniform definitions apply, realize that there is a huge difference between advisors who are willing to take moral, ethical, or legal responsibility for their actions and those who aren't. Many high-level advisors have a written commentary regarding how they view their responsibilities. A good example of this is the case study on the next page—*Advisors Take Responsibility*.

You May Be a Fiduciary: Things to Know if You Are

Some people reading this book may be on a board of directors, an investment committee, or an oversight committee of a company or charitable institution. Depending on the type of company or committee you are associated with and the laws that apply to that group, you may have fiduciary responsibility and could be held accountable and liable for the appropriateness of the investments under your care. Also, lack of financial knowledge may not be a viable legal defense. If you hold this type of position, be sure to check with your attorney for legal liability.

The following federal and state standards deal with key financial responsibility issues.

- Uniform Management of Institutional Funds Act (UMIFA) for Endowments and Foundations
- Uniform Management of Public Employee Retirement System Act (UMPERS also known as MPERS) for Public Funds
- Employee Retirement Income Security Act (ERISA) for Defined Benefit, Contribution and Profit Sharing Plans
- Uniform Trust Code (UTC) for trusts
- Uniform Prudent Investors Act (UPIA) for all individual investors (Uniform state laws passed in most states – as of this writing.)

In addition, organizations within the financial services industry have laid out non-regulatory standards that advisors are strongly encouraged to follow. For example, The Foundation for Fiduciary Studies has created Uniform Fiduciary Standards of Care. These very specific standards for dealing with the high net worth market are currently being drafted.

Michael Searcy is an Accredited Investment Fiduciary (AIF) with the Foundation for Fiduciary Studies, an organization that recently published *Prudent Investment Practices: A Handbook for Investment Fiduciaries.* The handbook outlines 27 practices that define a prudent investment process for fiduciaries. Mike offers an explanation of what a fiduciary is, plus outlines some of the standards that fiduciaries should consider.

According to Mike, "A fiduciary is someone who is responsible for the ongoing management of another individual's or entity's funds. This includes investment advisors, investment committee members, and trustees. Investment advisors are people who provide comprehensive and continuous investment advice. Therefore, by definition, we are fiduciaries. We have both a legal and ethical responsibility to our clients."

ADVISORS TAKE RESPONSIBILITY

Craig Pluta, Co-Founder the ReAct! Group, discusses a case involving a client who almost over-invested in equities, but was convinced by Craig and his partner, Chris Doughty, to be more conservative and also allocate a percentage of his assets to bonds. Up to this point he had only owned equities. This is a very important point regarding fiduciary responsibility.

Craig comments that the reason the man finially allocated some of his money to bonds was not just because he and Chris appealed to the logic of financial right and wrong, but also because they sat there and argued with him and reminded him that it was his retirement that was at stake. They asked a series of probing "what if" questions regarding different economic and market scenarios. When the market correction in 2000 arrived, it made a huge difference. That's the type of bond they have with their clients.

Craig says, "I think it's not that different from when our clients parented their kids and told them, 'I'm making you do something because I know this is the right thing for you. You may not agree with me, but you've got to trust me.' In a sense it's the same thing with clients and their advisors, we've just reversed the roles. Even though most of our clients are older than us, we're taking on a responsibility, similar to parental responsibility. It's called fiduciary responsibility. And we're saying to them, 'You can't just use your gut. Some of what you need to do is actually counterintuitive. We have to be resolute when we know intellectually that it's the right course of action. The financial media often compounds the problem by leading you to believe that good decisions are just about having information, after all we live in the information age, but having information is clearly different than applying the wisdom of how to use it and making good decisions."

Craig occasionally tells a client that he's sure that they could go to the Internet and find step-by-step instructions on how to perform open-heart surgery. The information is definitely there. Yet he doubts that anyone is going to crack open the chest of a loved one and actually do the surgery. Again, it's about wisdom, understanding how to use the information, and caring enough to argue for the right course of action.

Craig and Chris sum up their opinion on this important subject by saying that they believe if anyone in the financial industry is not going to act in a legal fashion, or is in the business just to do sales, he or she shouldn't be in the industry. "Fortunately, those people typically wash out of the industry," Craig says. Unfortunately, he adds, they leave a wake of damage behind them. "The moral and ethical responsibility is extremely important. You have a moral responsibility to the people whose money you're working with, especially in our field where we specialize in retirees and work with their life savings. This is all the money that's going to sustain them from this point all the way to the end. It must help them satisfy their desires for their legacy as well as gifting money to their kids and charity – whatever their wishes are. So there is an absolute responsibility to do everything you can to make all the best decisions and help them move in the direction they need to go."

"It means putting your best foot forward every day and not asking the question, 'Is this the best thing for me?' but "Is this the best thing for the client?'" he says.

As a fiduciary, there are certain standards of care that must be adhered to:

- Know standards, laws, and trust provisions.
- Diversify assets to the specific risk/return profile of the client.
- Prepare investment policy statements.
- Use 'prudent experts' and document due diligence.
- Control and account for investment expenses.
- Monitor the activities of the 'prudent experts.'
- Avoid conflicts of interest and prohibited transactions.

Continuing, he says, "Individuals who are on a board of directors, for example, may be fiduciaries. Clients who have fiduciary responsibility should be concerned about all of the same standards that we [Searcy Financial Services] adhere to. As trustees or board members, they are responsible for all of the same issues. If the entity for which they have a fiduciary responsibility is required to adhere to 'Safe Harbor' provisions, they must:

1. Use 'prudent experts.'
2. Follow a due diligence process when selecting 'prudent experts.'
3. Give 'prudent experts' investment discretion.
4. Have 'prudent experts' acknowledge co-fiduciary status in writing.
5. Monitor the activities of the 'prudent experts.'
6. Avoid conflicts of interest and prohibited transactions.

SOME EXAMPLES

Example #1: Michael J. Searcy of Searcy Financial Services, Inc. was at a meeting after an investment committee had interviewed several advisor candidates. Mike's company was selected as an advisor and co-fiduciary because everyone else came in and told the investment committee how they were going to manage the money, what returns they hoped to achieve, how they would allocate assets, etc. Mike told the committee how he was going to examine their processes and procedures and help them set up the fiduciary standards that they needed to follow because that was something they should be doing and were not.

Example #2: William Baker of William Baker & Associates, Inc. helps end this chapter by giving insight into his personality and on the issue of fiduciary responsibility. He says, "I started out in high school with the idea of becoming a physician before being detoured from that profession with an appointment to the U.S. Naval Academy. As a naval aviator, I flew search and rescue missions in Vietnam. Those younger days reinforced my basic nature, which was to help others. Flying Search and Rescue missions off the carriers in Vietnam provided a different realm for helping others and managing risk but it was still good carry over experience for the investment advisory business. Inherent in carrier flight operations is a great deal of trust. There are a lot of moving parts to that operation and the glue that makes it work is the trust that everyone is doing their job and looking out for the other person irrespective of rank or rate.

Recently there have been great numbers of the investment public and investment professionals let down by multiple layers of fiduciary gatekeepers (federal and state legislators, regulators, boards of directors, corporate executives, investment bankers, Wall Street fundamental researchers, accounting professionals, legal professionals, mutual fund companies, brokerage houses, etc.). A great deal of devastation has been done as a result of some of the fiduciary breaches – breaches in trust – that we've experienced.

So yes, I do feel that I have ethical, as well as regulatory responsibility to my clients. To fulfill that responsibility to the best of my ability requires continual training for my associates and me, continual improvement in our risk management techniques, and more effective servicing of our clients by providing the best tools, research, procedures, and technology.

I think clients and their advisors should be tuned in to stewardship issues – their own as well as the firms, corporations, and mutual funds in which they invest. Morningstar, Inc., a leading provider of independent research, recently initiated a stewardship rating for mutual funds and stocks. That is a good first step with the private sector getting into the game of helping the investing public."

In Conclusion

Do you want an advisor who is willing and capable of being a steward for your money? Do you have the desire to work with such people and have the personality characteristics that would allow you to do so? If so, you are lucky. If not, then during your search for the "right" financial advisor, keep these requirements foremost in your mind during the interview process.

◆◆◆

Puckett on Integrity

"A line in the movie, The Godfather, said, 'It ain't personal, it's business.' I adamantly disagree. When your business is wealth management, it definitely is personal.

At our firm, we strive to be excellent wealth managers and there can be no excellence without integrity. It means being brutally honest with our clients and ourselves at all times. It means doing what we say we'll do. It means being trustworthy, reliable, competent and above all, caring. Every strategy we craft for a client is no more or less than what we would do with our own money. Wealth management is (and should be) 'personal'-not 'simply business.'"

Brian W, Puckett, JD, CPA/PFS
Brian Puckett Retirement Advisors, LLC

Chapter 12

SYCHRONIZED and SYNERGETIC TEAMS

PROCES**S**: Synchronize

- To be simultaneous.
- To cause to occur at the same time.
- Concurrence of events.

PROCES**S**: Synergy

- Cooperative interaction among groups that creates an enhanced combined effect.

The rewards of working with an accomplished high-level advisor and other high-level professionals (attorneys CPAs, realtors, business valuation specialists, insurance agents, etc.) as part of a formal or informal alliance are invaluable. These professionals can constitute a comprehensive wealth management team. Unfortunately, many financial representatives from a variety of financial service firms claim to be members of an effective team – leading to confusion among investors and the possible selection of a poor team. Separating the wheat from the chaff is quite simple if you're willing to do some preliminary work and ask a few questions. Just remember that when you search for a financial advisor or team, make sure you search for the characteristics and attributes presented within these pages.

A Complete Team

Your current accountant, attorney, and insurance

specialist should be brought into the advisor's network of professionals. After all, high-level advisors welcome the opportunity to work with other professionals, provided those professionals are willing to be collaborative and put their egos aside to create an optimal plan for your benefit. If you don't have an attorney who specializes in estates, for example, the financial advisor will be able to recommend one. Sometimes the estate attorney may be a member of the advisor's internal team or, in most cases, an outside strategic alliance. A strategic alliance is a relationship between two or more professionals or firms that provide supplemental professional services to the advisor. Accountants and attorneys with specialized knowledge are the most common examples.

Eric Hutchinson tells clients that they should have a competent team of advisors as a way to run their lives more successfully. He describes a good team as having a financial advisor, a CPA, and a tax or estate attorney, as a minimum. And, depending upon circumstances, there could be different types of professionals on the team such as a banker, or an insurance agent to help protect them against various risks.

Eric says that he and his group encourage communication between team members. "We actually talk to their CPAs, their attorneys, and very often we will go with the client to an attorney meeting to discuss, for example, their estate plan." Eric explains that his team has already held the values and big

A COORDINATED EFFORT

Mike Piershale of Piershale Financial Group uses two attorneys to handle specific estate and trust issues.

"I work with two different attorneys whom I believe are very personable and very, very good. Their primary businesses are estate planning.

"Because these attorneys are so busy, I don't have them in on the initial meetings. Instead, I give the client basic estate planning advice and then send them to an attorney to get into more details and draft the documents."

When clients who already have an estate plan come to Mike, he will look over the documents, find out when it was last updated, and gather other pertinent information. If the clients need legal work, Mike will suggest they go to their own attorney if he or she has estate planning experience. In many cases, however, the clients have lost contact with their former attorneys and do not know how to find someone who is competent.

[Author's Note: Looking in the *Yellow Pages* is not the best way to find a competent professional, yet that is what many people do if they do not get a referral from someone they trust.]

In such cases, Mike will refer them to one of the attorneys he knows. The attorney then makes the final recommendation to the client.

picture conversation and have probably assembled most of the information the attorney will ask for. "So, with the client's permission, we provide that information to their attorney. For example, the tax attorney may need specific information. Rather than the client going through additional checklists and questionnaires, we hand the attorney a file which contains most of the answers. It makes their job easier, and allows them to focus on the real issues."

For example, although Tom Gau of Oregon-Pacific Advisors has tremendous knowledge and experience, he doesn't handle long-term care cases often enough to consider himself an expert in this area. Therefore, he refers such cases to a strategic alliance member who is a specialist in that field. Similarly, he often works with a specific attorney. Says Tom: "I'm not licensed to practice law and, therefore, I use an attorney to write up a legal document, such as a will, living trust, or power of attorney. The attorney isn't on my staff, but he's located two blocks away from here, and he is someone whom we feel comfortable relying on."

The point is, the high-level financial advisor has a network of high-level professionals to draw upon. As Bill Baker says, "After you work with various professionals within the community, you get a feel for who's reliable, who's responsible, and whom you are comfortable working with."

However, high-level advisors and their teams are often able to comment on, or help evaluate the documents prepared by other professionals. Many of the advisors commented that they have a number of clients with estate plan documents drawn by attorneys who are not experts in estate planning; these documents leave "something to be desired." (The same is true for taxes, insurances, etc. because the primary financial advisor is the one who looks at the big picture.) Fortunately, high-level advisors and their staffs see so many documents brought to them by their clients that they can spot many of the errors. So, keep in mind that if a professional is not regularly working with the particular issues you need addressed, it is usually wiser to find someone who is an expert in that area. For example, Chris Doughty says they are very careful who they work with because they have found that only one out of 20 attorneys regularly deals with the nuances of an Inherited IRA.

Another problem with documents could be that the "cookie cutter" estate plan hasn't been customized to meet the specific needs or desires of the client. Advisors walk a thin line by bringing it to the attorney's attention, especially if they rarely work with that attorney. Often advisors are already familiar with the competency levels of these professionals because they work with them often.

Don't All Financial People Have a Team to Rely on?

Absolutely not! Many financial representatives profess to be part of a formal team because they can tap into the resources of the entire firm. In reality, they often are individuals who offer the services of others – what we'll call "pseudo teams." A pseudo-team is one in which a financial representative is affiliated with other professionals in theory, but not in practice. For example, the financial representative does not actually have ongoing contact or a strong relationship with such professionals as tax, retirement, investment, or estate specialists. While they may ask these other professionals specific questions about your case, there may not be ongoing collaboration for your benefit.

For example, the estate planning department at a financial services firm may have 10 attorneys who can assist the sales representatives. The attorney who answers a question for the advisor today may not be the same attorney who answers a question for the advisor tomorrow, even though the question may be for the same client. In situations such as this, the departmental attorney may not be fully informed of your long-term goals and objectives, does not know what your dreams and aspirations are, and probably has no idea about your tax situation or real estate holdings. Yet he or she is giving advice that may affect your future.

Not All Teams Are Created Equal

Here are some questions you should ask an advisor to find out if they are part of a real or a pseudo team.

- How long has his or her "dedicated"[1] team worked together?
- How did they get together and why? (The answers will offer excellent insight into their structure and values.)
- Who are the other team members? What are their qualifications? Are they "exclusive" or "dedicated" to the team or do other financial representatives share their services? Ideal teams have "dedicated personnel."
- If the prospective advisor works within a larger firm, ask for specific background information about departmental representatives they work with on complex problems. (Most financial representatives in large firms deal with whatever tax expert or attorney happens to be available. By asking for specific biographical information and other specifics about the person, you'll know whether their "expert" is someone they've had numerous interactions with or is just another name in a large corporate directory.)
- What are their professional designations, certifications, and experience?
- What are their professional alliances outside of the firm? Your advisor should be familiar with the personal details of these alliance members and if you call that outside professional, he or she should be able to sing the praises of the advisor.
- What is their exact process for handling complex situations? Ask if

[1] Dedicated refers to personnel who work exclusively for the team. This can also be referred to as an "internal" team.

they could provide some case studies.

- What are their compensation practices? Do they share revenue? If so, is the revenue sharing in the form of referral fees or split commissions?
- How are all team members trained, and what inter-disciplinary cross-training do they undergo each year?

The Golden Rolodex: Going Beyond Professional Alliances

Good professionals from all disciplines create a network of people they can rely upon. Financial advisors and, yes, even financial sales representatives, are often able to help clients by referring them to other good product and service providers. For example, Craig Pluta says he can even direct clients to a good ocean cruise broker— the man happens to be one of his clients. Need a good roofer? Craig has referred several people to one he knows; and his clients have been very pleased. How about a physician?

The network of professionals an advisor can refer you to may surprise you. While it may seem unusual for an advisor to refer you to someone who is not linked to the financial services industry, Craig feels this is what friends and family members do. "If we know someone who is good, reliable, competent, caring, etc., we let our other friends know and become a resource for their clients in many areas," he says.

Cella Quinn says she has helped clients find jobs, "Send me a resume, and I'm good at finding someone a job. I have a huge network."

Mark Little has gone a step further to create a unique service for his clients and friends. He says he doesn't like salespeople to pressure him when he buys a car – neither do some of his clients. So, he has worked out a deal with a car buying service: For a flat fee, he and his clients provide the general parameters of what they want in their new car, and the service will do the searching, the comparison shopping, negotiation, and all of the other things associated with buying a car. All Mark and his clients have to do is test drive a car and make the final decision as to whether or not they want to purchase it. The service will even arrange for them to borrow the car overnight to see if they really like it. As Mark says, "When it comes time to actually buy the car, the buyers just show up at the dealership, sign the necessary paperwork, and drive off."

T.E.A.M.ing for Success

The acronym T.E.A.M. stands for Together Everyone Achieves More, an attitude promoted by many business organizations, followed by few, and rarely implemented effectively. Often personal and personnel issues get in the way of creating highly effective teams. Organizations that have highly effective teams are to be applauded, rewarded, and emulated. Such is the case with the teams that back the advisors featured in this book.

What is a Team?

The dictionary definition of team is, "a group of persons joined together in an action..." Teamwork is a "coordination of effort."

A great team is comprised of great people. During interviews, the advisors in this book told many wonderful stories of team members going the extra mile for their clients and making a difference in people's lives.

While the primary advisor may have the knowledge, none of these advisors could accomplish their tasks if it were not for all of the people supporting them and doing all of the day-to-day details that allow each system to run effectively. In many cases, team members are the advisors' eyes and ears. It's no wonder that each advisor had so many good things to say and placed such a high value on team services.

However, they didn't become team members by accident. Advisors are quite careful about whom they associate with. Whether a strategic partner or a staff member, each advisor searches for key characteristics that will match his or her business model. No one can afford to associate with someone who isn't client-centric, who doesn't share the same values, and who isn't willing to go the extra mile for their clients.

Michael Searcy says that when it comes to selecting an associate, he considers the attitude of the person. "We want somebody who has a servant's heart, somebody who is willing to do whatever it takes, someone who wants to improve their lot in life, someone who is conscientious, somebody who gets along with the other team mates, somebody who fits into our family atmosphere and corporate culture, and somebody who has the basic technical competence we need," he says. Mike says at one time he focused more on technical competencies, and it ended up being disastrous. He has since learned that the right attitude is essential. "You can teach somebody what he or she needs to know if they have the right attitude; but it's almost impossible to change someone's attitude," he says.

Questions to Ask Your Advisor

During initial and subsequent conversations with your advisor, or advisor candidate, make sure you ask about his or her support staff. You'll probably get some standard background information, but dig deeper and ask the advisor for a couple of circumstances in which staff members have done something special. If you get an almost immediate answer and the advisor "brags" about the staff member, this is a positive indication.

Also, listen to the pronouns the advisor uses in describing the business and the services offered. Are the pronouns primarily, "me, myself, and I" or do they include "we and us"? The combination of both indicates the advisor goes beyond looking at himself or herself and is team-oriented.

Other things to look for regarding internal teams include:

- Are team members listed or pictured on a company brochure?
- Are they listed on some sort of organizational or responsibility chart?
- Were you introduced to the team members you'll be interacting with?
- Do they seem friendly and eager to help you, both in person and on the phone?
- Do they handle problems or answer your questions promptly?
- Do they have their own business cards?
- Do you get calls from people on the team, not just the advisor?

A "yes" answer to questions such as these indicates an integrated, functional team working in a collaborative manner. Having an effective team is another characteristic of high-level advisors.

In Conclusion

By working with associates that have the right attitude and the knowledge to supplement the advisor's practice, a synergy occurs in which the whole is definitely greater than the sum of its parts. A financial advisor must be able to work efficiently and harmoniously with team members in order to provide exemplary service to clients.

◆◆◆

Piershale on Integrity

"I believe there are principles of human effectiveness in our world that operate across all societies. These principles are, in my opinion, laws that cannot be violated any more than the law of gravity without suffering consequences. Stephen Covey, the popular author of *Seven Habits of Highly Effective People,* calls them 'timeless universal principles of human effectiveness.' Jesus Christ made the statement, 'You will know the truth and the truth will set you free.' And I believe this was in reference to these same timeless universal principles.

One such law has to do with honesty and integrity. While dishonesty may result in people getting something they desire, eventually it will lead to both a lack of personal fulfillment, as well as ultimate negative consequences in their lives.

I have learned that it is important to be truthful and honest, not just in the bigger things but even in the smaller things. Besides fostering positive consequences in both our lives and in the lives of others, I believe integrity is simply good for business. When people know you are going to be truthful and honest even in the little things, you have just eliminated the greatest barrier to effective client-advisor relationships which is lack of trust."

Mike Piershale, Registered Principal
Raymond James Financial Services, Inc.

Chapter 13

Planning and Investments

"If you fail to plan, you plan to fail."

—unknown

You've read about situations in which people, similar to yourself, have experienced financial or legal difficulties because of their own errors (such as making erroneous assumptions, failing to follow advice) or because they relied on advice from less-than-competent individuals. Fortunately, many of these situations can be avoided or resolved when an advisor is able to spot a mistake and employ a strategy to save the day. Unfortunately, the interviews with advisors in this book also provided numerous examples of prospective clients asking for the advisor's help when it was already too late. Often the client had already suffered major consequences.

Conversely, you've read about situations in which the advisor has created an optimal solution because there was time to plan and implement a strategy.

This chapter is divided into three major sections:

1. Planning Strategies
2. Investment Strategy Tactics and Possible Pitfalls
3. Market Wisdom and Mistakes to Avoid

Financial Planning Versus Investments

Financial planning and investments can, in some ways, be considered the two sides of a coin – it's not one *or* the other, it's one *and* the other. You can have a great return on your money, but if you pay a large portion of it for taxes because something wasn't titled properly, it was for naught. Conversely, if you have a financial plan that calls for a certain growth rate, failure to attain the needed investment returns can prevent you from attaining your long-term goals and objectives.

After you and your advisor agree on a financial plan that determines your overall strategy (that's one side of the coin), your financial investments, businesses, and real estate become some of the vehicles you can use to maintain or increase your wealth (that is the other side of the coin).

I. Planning Strategies and Examples

This first section identifies some common financial planning errors made by people who have good intentions, but lack knowledge and experience.

Financial planning can be a complex undertaking fraught with potential traps. An advisor's job is to steer you through the maze and help you avoid the many landmines that exist. There are legal, investment, and tax issues that must be appropriately handled.

Remember that in all aspects of life – health, relationships, business, and certainly financial planning and investments – "an ounce of prevention is worth a pound of cure."

Unfortunately, investors who try to do some or all of the jobs on their own, despite their best intentions, can create unforeseen problems.

Errors people make when giving large monetary gifts or inheritances include: Not considering the ramifications of the gift, and being unaware of the problems the gift can pose. Recipients may not know how to handle the transfer of assets and could do what they think is "intuitively right" when, in reality, it is legally wrong. They may not be financially or emotionally ready to handle large sums of money.

Many people who come into new wealth lose it all within a few years because they don't know how to manage it. They can make poor financial decisions, from buying inflated real estate to funding various businesses or schemes. After all, they have money to burn. Some get involved in drugs, purchase extravagant gifts, pay off loans for friends, buy expensive cars and boats, take hordes of friends on vacation, or just lose their incentive to work. It's no wonder the money disappears so quickly.

The moral of the story is, if you want to fund a certain project, take care of a person's long-term medical expenses, or give a financial gift, your advisor can usually craft a solution that will help you accomplish your objectives. That solution may include trusts, family legacy planning, and education, to name just a few. An advisor will look at a problem from various angles and then provide an appropriate solution.

Case Study #1, provided by Tom Gau, Oregon Pacific Financial Advisors, highlights the benefits of getting a comprehensive financial analysis. Tom tells about clients who lost a substantial sum in taxes because their tax preparer neglected to take into consideration one very important item: Case Study # 2 provided by Mike Piershale [page 120], highlights the wisdom and experience gained from having a high-level advisor.

CASE STUDY #1

Years ago, Bill and Mary, who are residents of Oregon, purchased real estate for $200,000 in California (a community property state), therefore, each had a $100,000 cost basis. Over the years, the property appreciated to more than $1 million. When Bill died Mary wanted to sell the property for $1 million. Typically in a situation such as this, half the appreciation goes to the decedent and half to the surviving spouse. The decedent's appreciation is part of the estate and is handled separately. The wife then had to pay taxes on $400,000, which was considered her profit (half the sale proceeds minus her half of the original cost).

Tom Gau, Oregon Pacfic Financial Advisors, says if her Oregon-based accountant had known California laws, they could have provided her with better alternatives. In fact, Mary would not have had to pay taxes at all. Instead, a simple solution would have been to prepare a community property agreement in California. This would have caused both of them to receive a step-up in basis to $1 million, and the wife would not have had to pay any additional taxes at the time of sale.

Tom says he has learned many other ways to proactively avoid tax devastation, depending on the investor's particular situation. He suggests that investors find a comprehensive planner to look for their "weakest links." For example, you can hold great investments and have a good retirement plan, but if you forget to pay your medical premium or have an accident on an uninsured ATV, that could be your weakest link and could cause much grief. Therefore, he adds, "Find someone who can intelligently look at your total picture."

Choices, Choices Everywhere

George Jackson says people often know they need certain financial and estate planning procedures done, but they are not sure what or how to do them. He and his team help people make needed changes. "We facilitate change," he says. "We do it really well and make it as painless as possible so clients are not stressed. When we handle their investments, we'll do a lot of additional work without charge." Whether through tax planning or estate planning, George will make sure things are structured properly, and do so with minimal time and effort on the client's part.

"Many times people are like deer caught in a headlight. They don't know who to go to for help and are paralyzed with choices. They know there are a lot of attorneys out there, but they don't know which one to use." Because of George's long-time experience, he knows which attorneys to use. "I know

> **CASE STUDY #2**
>
> In his experience, Mike Piershale, Raymond James Financial Services, has found that trust departments in local banks can sometimes be very complacent in overseeing their clients' portfolios. Mike states, "We have had instances in which clients of ours have had special trust accounts being handled by local banks, and have elected to transfer those accounts to us because of dissatisfaction with the results. They felt, in some instances, that the bank was ignoring investment strategies that these clients felt should be considered. In some cases, clients felt the bank never called or offered to update them on their performance. When we take over such accounts, I normally find the need to make several changes in cooperation with the clients. In some cases, I have found that local trust departments have overlooked the value of purchasing life insurance particularly inside a Generation-Skipping Trust to ensure an inheritance for the grandchildren regardless of investment performance."

who is good and who isn't. And, if we don't have the expertise to handle something, we'll refer it to an expert who excels in that particular field," he says.

Taxes, insurance, investments, and legal issues must all be taken into consideration when creating a plan for you to achieve your goals. It can be intimidating and financially dangerous if you go it alone or don't choose the right advisors. Of course, doing nothing can be even more dangerous.

Once an overall game plan has been established, the advisor will help you fund the plan through various investment alternatives. The next two sections look at the art and science of investing in the financial markets by considering both the opportunities and dangers associated with investing.

II. Investment Strategies, Tactics, and Pitfalls

Investments are one of the prime vehicles, including legal and tax strategies, used in the financial plan to help you attain your goals.

Investment strategies, tactics, and pitfalls are the subject of thousands of books, courses, and publications. Here, some of the key strategies and tactics employed by the advisors featured in this book will be mentioned. In addition, they will point out common investment errors to avoid.

Advisors usually recommend investment strategies to clients as part of the overall solution. Advisors have systems in place to evaluate the investments they recommend and to make sure that the investment benchmarks are being attained. If something isn't going well, they will quickly know it and initiate a contingency plan.

Many of our featured advisors don't pick the individual securities for their clients -- they have partners or associates (internal or external) that specialize in that. It's vital in any team approach that each person knows his or her own strengths and plays to that strength. It's also important that they work with others to supplement their capabilities. This is the synergy and synchronization described in the previous chapter.

For example, the team at Hutchinson/Ifrah is divided into two primary groups: the financial advisory team headed by Eric Hutchinson, and the investment team headed by Patrick Ifrah. Eric says he and other members of the advisory team don't make day-to-day investment decisions for their clients. Instead, they work with clients to gather information, create a financial plan, and make strategic decisions on the overall asset allocation. Then Patrick and his team become responsible for making decisions concerning assets to buy, hold, or sell.

Eric adds that Patrick is very good with handling the research, monitoring, and other money management issues. "He and his team are good at what they do and the long term results speak for themselves.."

The Hutchinson/Ifrah process is very structured, from its use of technology, to its investment monitoring, to its speed on detecting when something is off track. For example, if a particular mutual fund, purchased to accomplish a specific investment objective, isn't on track, then the team will quickly move to initiate a contingency plan so the client's objectives are not jeopardized. Essentially, if one investment doesn't go in the direction they want it to go, they'll exchange it for one that will.

Eric says the firm's internal organizational structure allows team members to use their unique abilities and passions—and for their clients to benefit from people performing at their best.

In contrast, George Jackson and Brian Puckett are the primary investment managers at their respective firms. Both use very rigorous, objective criteria to systematically follow the market and make individual stock selections.

Example #1: George Jackson of Jackson Retirement Planning believes in "trend investing." Rather than relying on stock market gurus or third-party forecasts, George lets the market tell him what is going on. He says trends persist much longer than people think. In fact, based on his studies, trends typically last three to six years. Of course he promotes a diversified portfolio so his clients aren't hurt if he is wrong. "You have to be very humble when you invest in the market," he says.

Most of George's clients are wealthy and one of their biggest fears is losing wealth, so he tries to protect them on the downside as best as he can. He accomplishes that protection with a well-diversified portfolio made up of assets that, historically, have not gone down significantly. For example, between August 31, 2000 and October 8, 2002, Intel fell 82.5 percent. "That's a risky asset. And, most importantly, if it fell that hard before, it can do it again," he says.

In addition, George says it is important to eliminate, or at least reduce, the emotional aspect of investing, and the best way to do this is to reduce the volatility of the portfolio.

Example No. 2: Brian Puckett has a similar approach. His mantra is, "Manage money for the downside, and let the upside take care of itself." He will "stress test" the client by running different scenarios past them. This helps him determine what a client's risk tolerance really is. If a client can withstand a 10 percent downward movement of his or her portfolio within a 12-month period, then he'll use a certain mixture of stocks, bonds, real estate, managed futures, etc. If the client can handle a 15 percent downward movement on a temporary basis, it will lead to an entirely different investment mixture.

When determining the investment mixture, Brian often searches for undervalued situations. He typically gets into an investment early and realizes that patience is required for his clients to reap the rewards of overweighting undervalued situations. In addition, "We don't go hog wild and load the boat on any one investment. We stay sufficiently diversified at all times," he says

Brian says that one of the secrets to investing is that there *are* no secrets. "You can look back on history and get a pretty fair idea of what a client can reasonably expect as far as the long-term returns of various capital markets[1]."

Brian makes an astute observation as he paraphrases what investment expert Warren Buffett says: "Wall Street is a very expensive place to try to figure out who you are and what you want to accomplish."

"There's a lot of truth to that," Brian says. "In order to be successful in the world of investing you really need to have clarity about what you're trying to accomplish and you need to have a very disciplined process to help you navigate the complex world of finance. That process must be well grounded, researched, and time tested – one that you believe in so that you don't get whiplashed one way or another by movements in the market or be swayed with the emotions of fear or greed that are constantly being touted over the internet, CNBC, or any other popular media." Brian advocates a disciplined process, which he believes is essential to creating a solid framework that takes a client from where they are right now to the place that they want to be.

Some advisors opt to use money managers from mutual funds or other money management firms. The choice of manager depends on numerous factors. Essentially, your needs, goals, and risk tolerance determine which money management services are most appropriate for you. Then each of

[1] Past performance of any financial product is not indicative of future results. We encourage you to consult your financial advisor to discuss these things.

the services is rated against a number of parameters and statistics such as performance history, investment style, and depth of experience.

An advisor since the early 1970s, Cella Quinn specializes in hiring the brains and talent of mutual fund managers. She relates a story about how and why she became involved with mutual funds, and also explains the approaches that have enabled some of her clients to become millionaires.

In the early part of her career Cella tried to convince clients to purchase relatively unknown ("wallflower") stocks that had excellent market potential – "the same type of stocks that Warren Buffett was buying at that time," she says. In fact, Cella's office was next to the stockbroker who handled Warren Buffett's accounts. At that time, Mr. Buffett was well known, but had not yet attained superstar status. However, Cella learned some valuable lessons about buying "wallflower stocks" and about the psychology Mr. Buffett used when purchasing them.

At one point, she called up 100 clients and told them about five wallflower stocks of the type that Mr. Buffet was buying; yet only one of her clients was willing to purchase one of the five stocks at $12 per share. As fortune would have it, the price promptly went down to $9, and the client unhappily sold. (Eventually the stock went up to the mid $50 range.[1])

She says those who buy individual stocks rather than mutual funds tend to buy what she calls 'Homecoming Queens' which are companies like the dot.coms that are popular, have products that sizzle and who look good on the surface. They may or may not be actually making money. Homecoming Queens are perceived to be solid but oftentimes they are the riskiest because, Cella says, "When you buy what everyone else is buying, you are more likely to buy high and sell low. Yet, it's virtually impossible to convince clients to invest in unrecognized, undervalued stocks with low price/earnings ratios that have yet to be discovered."

Cella sees her job as being a wealth builder. How was she to do it if the only companies clients were willing to date were Homecoming Queens? It was the portfolio managers of the mutual funds who drooled over the chance to date/ invest in a company that was a wallflower.

Cella comments, "Fortunately, I have savvy clients who understand the advantage of funds. They like the fact that their money is professionally managed and the fact that they earn dividends and capital gains which compound whether the market is up or down. When the market is down, compounding really works as their reinvested dividends buy more shares — That's how and why I got into funds."

While each advisor can offer numerous examples of investment suc-

[1] Of course, not all mutual funds do as well. Also, the information provided in this chapter does not constitute investment advice and it should not be relied on as such. Past performance of any financial product is not indicative of future results. We encourage you to consult your financial advisor to discuss these things.

cesses and tragedies, he or she hastens to point out that the successes come from proven, disciplined approaches, while failure comes in a variety of ways. The next section offers advice on how to and how not to invest.

III. Market Wisdom and Mistakes to Avoid

Throughout this section are numerous italicized Wall Street adages that apply to the psychology of investing, such as: *"Most of us tend to be wrong most of the time, especially when we agree with one another."* We hope that these adages will reinforce the key point that investing should be based on logical, consistent, objective, systematic, proven systems, and that investors should avoid getting emotionally involved in the market. One of the best ways to do this is to use an advisor who is trained to be dispassionate and who has the experience to remain objective and systematic.

As human beings, it's easy to get "carried away with the crowd," whether it concerns stock market enthusiasm or despair. Investors are surrounded by advice – from the media, associates at the water cooler, and people at various parties who all seem to be making money. Michael Searcy warns people against the "if it is on TV, it must be true" mentality. He says that too often people do not perform their due diligence before acting on information they have heard. This is one of the reasons it is important to have an advisory team available to help ensure objectivity and employ

MUTUAL FUNDS

Cella Quinn, Cela Quinn Investment Services, recounts a situation in which a client, starting in 1983, put $2,000 into one of her recommended funds, and regularly added to the account. Their total investment was $686,000, most of it in later years after they sold their small business. By August 2005, the mutual fund accounts were worth $1.9 million.

An efficient way to determine whether you would have done better in mutual funds is to take the same amounts of money you invested in stocks on the same dates and plug it into the past performance software used by mutual fund companies. This gives you an apples-to-apples comparison of "What would have happened if...." Cella says many people hesitate letting her do this because "ignorance is bliss, they don't always want to know how much money they've lost by not going with funds." With the exception of one person who put his money into Berkshire Hathaway in the years when BRK trading range was $400 to $5,000 a share, she says her computations show that mutual funds almost always outperform a portfolio of individual stocks.

Cella believes that people are usually more willing to hold onto a mutual fund for the long term than they are individual stocks, hence they tend to do better in funds. The job of an advisor is not to micro-manage the funds by second guessing the portfolio manager but rather to very closely monitor the funds' performances. If the manager is seriously underperforming the benchmark index, a good advisor will find out why and then will counsel his or her clients about what is best for them.

Cella tells about a recent client, Tim, who received $10,000 when he was born which was invested in a well-known Chicago company. Fifty years later, Tim's portfolio suffered from what she calls the Enron Syndrome where he had most of his money in one stock. Tim explained how the value of this stock had grown from $10,000 to $195,000 and that he would never get rid of it. Cella then did a comparison of the stock versus a well-known growth and income fund. She found the same amount of money invested on the same day in a mutual fund would have grown to over $11 million.

Comparing the actual past return on investments is a useful tool for investors and can easily be done because of the extensive performance software that is available.

rigorous selection criteria.

Always remember, *"If you hear that 'everyone' is buying, ask who is selling?"* Far too many people get drunk on the excitement of making money in a bull market and start to believe that their superior skills and knowledge (or their stockbroker's) are responsible.

A good example of investor overconfidence was experienced during the bull markets of the late 1990s, 1980s, 1960s, and 1920s. During those times, many people decided it was "easy" to manage their own investments and that the stock market was the sure road to fame and fortune— that is, until the market turned downward. Perhaps they should have heeded the old Wall Street adage, *"Don't confuse brains with a bull market."*

Chris Doughty tells about a client who made a lot of money with high-tech stocks in the 1990s. After Chris and partner Craig Pluta educated him on stock market theory and practices, the client realized that the profits he experienced were the result of the bull market carrying him upward, and not his own brilliance in selecting stocks. Accepting that truth was critical to formulating a quality plan.

In a different situation, Yale Levey tells about a client who assumed that the exceptional performance Levey had obtained for his portfolio would continue indefinitely. Yale said he had to "reel him in a bit and alert him to the fact that it's not easy to do much better than the index[1] over the long run, and that it wouldn't be prudent to assume that we [Yale's team] would continually meet his lofty expectations."

Yale points out that part of his real value is to keep people from making disastrous decisions, like chasing unrealistic investment returns. This example demonstrates how a professional isn't blinded by his own reflected glory, but maintains balance, objectivity, and remains dispassionate.

Fortune Tellers and Stock Market Prognosticators

Thousands of people make their livings by generating commissions

[1] An Index is a portfolio of specific securities (common examples are S&P, DJIA, NASDAQ), the performance of which is often used as a benchmark in judging the relative performance of certain asset classes. Indexes are unmanaged portfolios and investors cannot invest directly in an index. Past performance is not indicative of future results.

or selling advisory newsletters that promote the concept of picking the right stocks and beating the market. Unfortunately, they often recommend the same few, popular stocks (what Cella Quinn calls the "Homecoming Queens").

Following their advice may be fine for that portion of your investments allocated toward speculating, but such advice generally offers little value to the real avenue for making money in the stock market, which is through asset allocation.

Asset allocation (allocating your portfolio holdings among various asset classes such as stocks, bonds and cash) accounts for more than 90 percent of the variability of a portfolio's performance. That revelation was given in "Determinations of Portfolio Performance II: An Update," a landmark study by Brinson, Singer, and Beebower, which appeared in the *Financial Analyst Journal* of May-June 1991. The study provided new insights for investors and investment professionals alike. It showed that only 4.6 percent of the entire portfolio return was due to security selection, 2.1 percent from market timing, and 1.8 percent from other factors.

Subsequent studies have provided similar results and have repeatedly shown that time in the market (that is, investing for the long-term) is another key ingredient for success. Asset allocation plus long-term investing maximizes your probability for success.

Why, then, is it that so many investors insist on the low-probability strategy of buying what everyone else is buying? Stock market history repeatedly demonstrates that crowd euphoria (unrealistic expectations) is greatest near the peak of a bull market. While the peaking stage of a bull market may last for months, this stage usually only represents 10 to 15 percent of the rise, with 85 to 90 percent of the bull market move having already been realized. It is at times like these that investment publications, newspapers, and newsletters are fueling the fire with headlines like, "Today's highs are tomorrow's lows," "We're in a new economy," "How high is up?" "We've only just begun," and "Happy days are here again." In response to this euphoria, ask yourself, "If everyone is buying, who is selling?" The answer usually is: the professionals.

The converse is true near the end of the bear market when the stock market magazines, reflecting the psychology of the crowd (which is usually wrong), has headlines like, "How far down can the market go?" "Can the market ever be revitalized?" "How to sell short," and "The end is near."

Ultimately, the "best" way to invest is still to take the conservative, long-term route with your important money – the majority of your investment funds – and to allocate those funds among different asset classes, that is, diversify. If you have extra money that you don't mind losing, go ahead and play the market. But, only play/speculate/gamble with that relatively small sum and no more. Then, if you are successful within the bull market you can say, "me too" when talking to other market "players." But, by being wise with how you've handled your important money, you can avoid that forlorn "me too" when everyone else is complaining about heavy losses.

Eric Hutchinson makes the point that part of an advisor's role is to manage expectations and to keep clients in realistic contact with what's happening in the world. He says, "If everyone else is losing 25 to 50 percent of their portfolio, and we only lose 1 or 2 percent, we're doing a heck of a job."

Diversify, diversify, diversify!

Objectivity

It also helps to be dispassionate about one's own money when making any type of investment. This allows you to evaluate your situation in an objective fashion and avoid the common emotions that lead to failure, including greed, fear, hope, lethargy, and falling in love with a stock. It also allows you to think of stocks, bonds and other financial investments as "tools" whose sole purpose is the generation or protection of investment capital. If one tool/stock doesn't work, then find another that will better suit your needs. You don't, of course, automatically get out of a stock because it hasn't performed – you re-evaluate it very carefully. After all, it could be a member of an industry group that is about to embark on its cyclical upward move.

Of course, we're not suggesting that you do it yourself. Advisors have the training, knowledge, special tools, access to specialized information, and the discipline to pick the appropriate investments, while remaining dispassionate.

As Craig Pluta says, "The problem is that I have yet to meet someone who could be truly dispassionate about their own money. That becomes a problem because they are not able to see the forest for the trees. Too often, doing the right thing is counter-intuitive. Rebalancing assets is such an example. We naturally want more of the winners and want to cut the losers, which is often the wrong thing to do. Being able to trim back from the asset classes that have already performed, and move that money to the side that has not yet performed – realizing that there are cycles in the market – is a very difficult thing to do. It just doesn't feel right to many people. Left to their own devices they will often do exactly the wrong thing."

At points like this, Craig says his team has trained itself to rely on their intellect and their ability to objectively analyze the situation using their ReAct! process. "It's times like this that having an objective third-party who has knowledge, training, and experience available to guide you is so important."

Mark Little offers a different perspective. He notes how people sell one mutual fund and get into another within a couple of years, instead of allowing the fund to run its natural course over a full market cycle, which usually takes three to five years. When Mark reviews a prospect's statement from five years earlier, he often finds they would have been better off if they had just held the fund for a longer period. The problem was that they let their emotions get in their way and didn't rely on a strategy that has a definite, proven methodology.

Cella Quinn tells about a businessman who became wealthy when shares of a small communications company skyrocketed from single digit to over $130. His net worth was $2 million plus, and his income was $1 million a year.

"Should I take my profit and pay all those taxes?" he asked her as they walked toward the golf course.

"How much do you need to live on?" she asked of this executive she barely knew.

"$350,000 a year."

Cella advised him to sell a portion of his portfolio and buy long-term governments to provide the income he needed. The businessman called back the next week and said, 'That's not a bad idea. I'll wait to sell until it hits $200 and then maybe I'll be your client." Since then he's watched it decline to $2 a share and now it is worth approximately $300,000. Instead of being able to retire, he's back at work.

Mike Piershale finds it rewarding to help new clients recover when their portfolios have been decimated due to poor management. He helps them through the use of sound portfolio management strategies. Mike states, "Particularly after the three-year bear market from 2000 through 2002, we had more than one retired couple make their way to our office who had lost a significant part of their portfolios. Many times, people had lost 40 to 50 percent. In cases like this, we found many couples were paralyzed with fear and didn't know which direction to take. They didn't want to get out of the market because they hoped to get their money back, but were afraid to stay in the market for fear of going from bad to worse."

In many cases Mike has found couples with far too much money not just in stock, but in stock that was too aggressive for their risk tolerance. Depending on the circumstances, Mike will use different strategies to get clients on the road to recovery. "Often," he comments, "we find that one of the most fundamental things we need to do is reduce the percentage of a portfolio that is in stock. We have had cases with as much as 70 to 90 percent of a portfolio in the stock market. We will also try to weight them a little heavier in large cap stocks that pay higher dividends; this can give them appreciation potential, but provide more stability in case of future market declines."

While some financial advisors in the industry might sometimes feel frustrated with unsophisticated investors, or investors that are slow to understand financial concepts, Mike Piershale enjoys the challenge of helping them learn. "I guess it's the school teacher in me," Mike states. "I taught high school juniors and seniors before I came into the financial business. I have always enjoyed seeing the light bulb go on when people learn something." One of the most common scenarios that Mike observes with unsophisticated investors is that they will be invested in portfolios of poorly performing stocks that they are reluctant to change. In these cases, Mike will patiently work with the investor, going through the portfolio to show him or her the reasons why a poorly performing stock may need to be sold. Mike will often suggest, in such cases, that the investor consider moving some or all of the assets into investments that will provide greater diversification and professional management.

Ouch!

"The stock market is that creation of man that humbles him the most."

Many investors who have lost money in the market now realize their strategic or tactical errors and are searching for an investment professional who can show them ways to achieve their goals.

The aftermath of poor investment decision-making is often emotional scarring and the desire to assign blame. Sometimes investors feel personal shame for their decisions or are embarrassed that they trusted someone who, in hindsight, was simply a great salesperson. A good advisor won't criticize you, but will help you identify and learn from your mistakes. They will help you outline your goals, craft an investment plan and find the right approaches so mistakes don't happen again.

If you want to invest like a professional, then you must have the required knowledge, technical abilities, and discipline to do the job – or hire somebody who does. If you hire somebody, then make sure you give him or her the authority and the time to do an effective job.

In Conclusion

"Those who do not learn from history are doomed to repeat it."

Many people mentally project the continuation of a trend – the market will continue to go up, inflation will remain high/low/stable, tax rates will remain the same, etc. Market sophisticates know that change is the only constant. Therefore, they have contingency plans, and are constantly monitoring the situation so that they can make the appropriate adaptations.

"No profession requires more hard work, intelligence, patience, and mental discipline than successful investing."

Use an advisor who can demonstrate success in the market through his or her investment processes.

◆◆◆

"I am still learning."

—Michelangelo

Chapter 14

The Importance of Advisor Education

If you walk into Brian Puckett's office you will see this simple, framed quotation from the Renaissance genius. It epitomizes Brian's passion for on-going professional development. It also represents the educational focus of the other advisors in this book.

The Value of Continuing Education

In this rapidly changing investment world, new products, services, and investment strategies are constantly being developed. While high-level advisors who hold industry designations have maintained stringent continuing education requirements for many years, as of this writing regulatory authorities have imposed minimal (and, rather nebulous) continuing education requirements on the balance of the financial services industry.

Regardless of an advisor's learning preference, many spend thousands of dollars and hundreds of hours each year in continuing education and professional development. They attend industry conferences, and/or take courses (certification or non-certification), and/or subscribe to magazines and professional journals, and/or purchase books relevant to their profession, and/or network with peers and professional colleagues.

Over the years, a number of financial industry

associations have been created. These associations focus on various aspects of the financial services industry and allow members to earn designations or certifications after completing a particular course of study. The Certified Public Accountant (CPA), Chartered Life Underwriter (CLU), Certified Investment Management Analyst (CIMA) and Certified Financial Planner (CFP) designations are some of the more common designations. Note: Later in this chapter is a list of many prominent designations and contact information for the sponsoring organizations.

Most of these industry designations require ongoing continuing education in order to maintain the designation or certification. To help you get a feel for the amount of study required, George Jackson says the continuing education requirement to maintain his CPA designation is 80 hours every two years. The CFA is about 50 hours a year. Some of the courses he takes apply to multiple designations. He says: "I like this business. I enjoy it. I'm always open to education." [In addition, George is a CLU and a Chartered Financial Consultant (ChFC).]

Many of the advisors interviewed reported that they spend upward of 20 percent of their time in educational activities.

"Sharpening the Saw"

Any advisor who goes beyond the norm to earn professional designations, and pursue educational opportunities, and who subscribes to a stringent code of ethics, should stand far above the others.

Stephen Covey in his book, *The 7 Habits of Highly Effective People*, noted that one of the key characteristics of top-level people in any profession (or for that matter, in life) is continuous personal and professional improvement – or what he calls "sharpening the saw."

A good example of advisors who do this are Chris Doughy and his partner Craig Pluta who subscribe to more than 20 different types of educational materials, not including scores of educational e-mails from industry groups and peers.

Another is Tom Gau, who subscribes to the *I.R.S. Private Letter Rulings* because it gives him a distinct advantage in tax law. As a result, he says he has been using tax strategies often years before those strategies become well-known and popular by the balance of the industry.

For discerning investors, the only competition for one high-level advisor is another high-level advisor. There are, literally, hundreds of thousands of less knowledgeable, non-credentialed, and less experienced advisors who may also be able to assist you in one way or another; but can you afford to take the chance?

Consider this: Would you take your brand new car to an auto mechanic who doesn't like to deal with those new-fangled, computer-chip thing-a-ma-bobbers? Would you want to retain an attorney who hasn't kept up with case law or go to a doctor who hasn't kept up with medical advances? Chances are, you wouldn't choose to go to any of them unless your needs were truly simple, or you didn't care what kind of service you received, or you had no choice.

It is hard to imagine any affluent investor using the services of anyone other than a high-level financial advisor when there is so much at stake.

"Who Knows What?" and "What Is Important to You?"

An advisor's experiences, designations, and the extent of continuing education are useful ways to judge his or her potential value as an advisor. Realize, however, that a designation or degree does not automatically equal competence and caring. You can only determine those traits through your due diligence, meeting the advisor, and working with him or her for a period of time. Ultimately you want someone who gets high ratings in each of the five continuums presented in Chapter 1.

CFP® designee Yale Levey gives this advice regarding designations: "At the very least the financial advisor should be a CFP or a ChFC so that they [clients] know the advisor has gone though extra, extensive training, and is required to stay on top of things in order to maintain the designation. It's not that advisors without letters after their name aren't going to be good—those letters wouldn't necessarily help the client to succeed. Clients are just stacking the odds in their favor by hiring advisors who have gone through that process—they're making it more likely that they'll get what they need."

Deciphering Alphabet Soup[1]

The list of financial services industry associations and organizations providing designations is so long that there is not room to list them all here. Each has different, yet overlapping, services. Depending on your financial needs, different designations, degrees or organizations would be more sought after than others. For example, if you are looking for portfolio management and evaluation services, consider a Certified Investment Management Analyst (CIMA), Certified Investment Management Consultant (CIMC) or Chartered Financial Analyst™ (CFA®).

For financial planning services, CFP, CPA, Chartered Financial Consultant (ChFC), and Chartered Life Underwriter (CLU) designations may be more helpful for your needs.

To learn more about each designation, including its educational requirements, code of standards/ethics, and practitioners in your area, call the organization(s) or visit their Web sites. The National Association of Securities Dealers (NASD) also offers a listing of designations it recognizes, with

1 Some people have so many designations after their name that it looks like alphabet soup. Yet, even a professional with dozens of designations may not be suitable for you.

Designation		Website	Telephone
AIF	Accredited Investment Fiduciary	www.cfstudies	412-741-8140
AIFA	Accredited Investment Fiduciary Auditor	www.cfstudies.com	412-741-8140
CFA®	Chartered Financial Analyst	www.aimr.org	800-247-8132
CFP®	Certified Financial Planner™	www.cfp.net	888-237-6275
CAP	Certified Advisor in Philanthropy	www.advisorsinphilanthropy.org	812-597-4251
ChFC	Chartered Financial Consultant	www.amercol.edu	888-263-7265
CIMA	Certified Investment Mgmt Analyst	www.imca.org	303-770-3377
CIMC	Certified Investment Mgmt Consultant	www.imca.org	303-770-3377
CIS	Certified Investment Strategist	www.imca.org	303-770-3377
CLU	Chartered Life Underwriter	www.amercol.edu	888-263-7265
CPA	Certified Public Accountant	www.aicpa.org	888-777-7077
CSA	Certified Senior Advisor	www.society-csa.com	888-653-1785
PFS	Personal Financial Specialist	www.aicpa.org	888-777-7077
RIA	Registered Investment Advisor	www.sec.gov/iard	202-942-0691

The National Association of Securities Dealers (NASD) offers a more comprehensive listing of designations if recognizes, with basic information about each. Visit http://www.nasd.org. Search for "designation." Select "What Does a Professional Designation Mean?" Then "view all designations in a printer-friendly chart."

basic information about each.

In addition to learning what the designations mean, we suggest that you ask the advisor to explain the course of study required for the designations or degrees they hold. Also ask about continuing education requirements or personal programs for ongoing education, what strengths and weaknesses the designation implies, and how it all applies to your particular needs.

Both George Jackson and Tom Gau suggest that you find someone who has a history of success in the specific areas you require. A person could suffer from "alphabet soup disease[2]" and may not be suitable for you if they don't have the specific and exact knowledge and experience you need.

Don't assume an advisor has specific knowledge; verify it – preferably in writing. Make sure they have "relevant" experience for your situation.

Mike Piershale says it is a mistake to insist that there is one superior path for training to be a good financial planner. A degree in business, combined with good company training is excellent preparation. Going through the CLU, ChFC or CFP programs can also provide excellent background. Mike also believes that it is very important for a well-rounded retirement planner to have a Series 7 license, as this is the license that allows broader flexibility and selection of investments for clients. "A Series 6," Piershale states, "just allows a financial planner to work with mutual funds and annuities, which may not be appropriate for every client."

Mike is a bit of a skeptic of those who suggest, however, that a basic designation somehow ensures greater competency. "Over the years, I have looked at many portfolios that were being managed by CFPs, CLUs, or MBAs that were mismanaged. For example, I have seen cases where people had been in poorly performing investments for years without being advised to move. I have seen half of a large portfolio in one stock, which violates basic rules of diversification. I have seen people in the 15 percent tax brackets who have all their bond money in tax-free bonds, which in my view is inappropriate for people in lower tax-brackets. The point is, investors should look beyond a basic designation and make sure they know something about their planner's personality, business history and track record." In addition to checking for an advisor's training, Mike also suggests that if an individual is ranked at the top of his or her company, he or she may be a good choice. As he says, "In my personal experience, I have never met anyone who was among the very top advisors in his or her company in terms of sales and production, that wasn't a person of excellence."

Mike makes a good point about top people in any company. Mike, himself, is on the Chairman's Council[1], which makes up his firm's top advisors in the United States; He is currently ranked 15th in the nation out of 3404 financial advisors in the Raymond James Financial Services division. We believe attaining these high levels of recognition is simply an outgrowth of spending years giving good financial planning advice and service. When you give good advice and good service, over time you create more demand.

A Variety of Eduational Methods

Not every advisor featured in this book has industry designations from one or more of these industry associations. Some prefer the self-study route because it allows them to pursue topics that are directly applicable to their clientele and because they already have an excellent network of professionals they can rely upon.

Remember that a designation does not automatically connote competence or caring. Chris Doughty says, "We have met numerous financial advisors with a lot of qualifications, and reviewed many of their plans. We've come to the conclusion that an advisor's technical competence doesn't necessarily help when the rubber meets the road. We found that training and designations aren't the key when it comes to working with people.

"We [advisors] don't have a tangible product. It isn't like trying to figure out who's got the best DVD player, or who makes the best television,

[3] Firms have various clubs or internal designations for advisors who consistently demonstrate business excellence. At most firms, the "Chairman's Club" (although some firms use different names) represents the most elite advisors within the firm. The "Chairman's Council" usually represents a special subsection of the Chairman's Club that has direct input to the firm's senior executives.

or has the best J.D. Power and Associates rating for quality in a car. This is really a business that's all about rapport, understanding people and who they really are, and meeting their needs."

An investor who was referred to Chris was dealing with a disastrous situation, and after several of hours of discussion at this first meeting, the investor's comment was, "I can't talk to my other guy like this. I feel like I can tell you anything."

Chris concludes that "It's unfortunate there isn't a designation for personal and interpersonal competencies, nor for creating a plan that matches the client." Ultimately it all comes down to the trust equation.

Also Look at Their Teams

Each advisor has spent considerable time and effort over the years developing staff members and outside relationships so that he or she can create the synergy described in Chapter 12. Rather than demanding a particular designation, make sure the advisor has access, though others, to the relevant information and expertise needed. Also, check on the continuing education that he or she and their team members go through each year.

Continuing education also applies to most or all staff members on an advisor's team. Michael Searcy makes continuing education part of the job description for all employees, and he bases part of their bonuses on completion of certain programs. He says, "It's part of my employment agreement, so it's not an option. If you're going to be in the business, you're going to be a professional in the business—in our firm anyway. I'm not hiring worker bees, I'm hiring partners. Eventually there may be a situation where we have three or four partners and just want worker bees. But the current people are the ones I'm grooming to eventually take over the company."

Also an advocate of team education, George Jackson, among other things, sends each of his staff members to the H&R Block income tax preparation course. He says the course allows them to prepare tax returns for their clients, and gives each staff member additional insight and understanding into the financial needs of their clients.

George also spends time personally conducting courses for his staff. As he says, "I try to educate them myself because I have a certain philosophy in the way I do things and want them to follow the processes I've developed so that we do business properly and efficiently."

Checking an Advisor's Disciplinary History

Before you interview an advisor, you should conduct a background check to get answers to questions such as: Are there any legal filings against the advisor? Has the advisor been sued? Has there been mismanagement within the firm?

The Central Registration Depository (CRD) is a computerized database that contains information about most broker-dealers and their representatives. You can find out if someone is properly licensed in your state, had run-ins with regulators, or received serious complaints from investors. You'll also obtain information on his or her educational backgrounds and job history on his or her Website.

Individual independent advisors or firms that are paid to give advice about investing in securities generally must register with either the SEC (if they manage more than $25 million) or the state securities agency where they have their principal place of business (if they manage under $25 million).

To find out about these advisors and managers and whether they are properly registered, read their registration forms (Form ADV). The Form ADV has two parts: Part 1 contains information about the advisor's business and whether he or she has had problems with regulators or clients. Part 2 outlines the advisor's services, fees, and strategies. Before you hire an investment advisor, always ask for and read both parts of the ADV or check online for the form.

You can get in touch with the state securities regulator through the North American Securities Administrators Association, Inc.'s Website. If the SEC registers the investment advisor, you can order a hard copy of Form ADV at a cost of 24 cents per page (plus postage) from the SEC.

The following websites and telephone numbers can help you in your search.

- **Certified Financial Planner Board of Standards, Inc.**
  Telephone: 888-237-6275 Website: www.CFP.net
- **North American Securities Administration**
  Telephone: 202-737-0900 Website: www.nasaa.org
- **National Association of Insurance Commissioners**
  Telephone: 816-842-3600 Website: www.naic.org
- **National Association of Securities Dealers Regulation**
  Telephone: 800-289-9999 Website: www.nasdr.com
- **Securities and Exchange Commission**
  Telephone: 202-942-7040 Website: www.sec.gov

Checking on an advisor's credentials and looking up any disciplinary history are important steps in the process. However, you may wish to go a step further. Also find out if the advisor has received any special recognitions in his or her field.

In Conclusion

As Michelangelo said, "I am still learning." Make sure your advisor is, too.

◆◆◆

Doughty on Integrity

"The client-advisor relationship starts with a mutual faith that what the client and advisor have agreed upon is true. For some, trust comes instantly as a gut feeling, while for others it is a process that can only mature over time. In either case, integrity is the essential component to the fulfillment and validation of that sacred trust. The end result is a 'knowing' by the client that his or her best interests are being sheparded every step of the way.

When an advisor works as a fiduciary, he or she must recommend what is in another person's best interest, removing the self from the equation. Integrity must permeate the practice of a financial advisor and is exemplified by his or her attention to the client's situation, by listening, showing empathy and providing solutions.

To us, Integrity is providing the best possible service to the best of our ability."

Chris Doughty
Co-founder, ReAct! Group
First VP, Ziegler Investment Services Group

Chapter 15

Client Education and Appreciation

A television commercial for Men's Wearhouse (clothing store) carries the tagline, "An educated consumer is our best customer." A high-level advisor has two similar desires: "An educated investor is the best client," and "An educated client is the best investor."

Advisors repeatedly emphasize the need for client education, the pleasure and personal satisfaction they receive from teaching people, and the mutual benefits derived from such education. All the advisors interviewed for this book make a concerted effort to enhance their clients' level of knowledge using a variety of methods such as: educational seminars, newsletters, personal meetings, meetings with a client's other professional advisors, meetings with family members, e-mails and anything else they can think of to assist their clients to learn and grow.

These advisors make the same commitment to educating clients as they do to ongoing professional development for themselves and their team. In many cases, client education goes beyond learning about finances.

Client appreciation is also discussed in this chapter. The advisors realize that they exist to help fulfill clients' needs. Clients and advisors are in a long-term partnership with each other, which calls for a lot of mutual respect and appreciation. Some advisors have gala client appreciation events, while others prefer more intimate one-on-one conversations over a nice dinner. Some clients express their appreciation with a heartfelt "thank you," while others refer family, friends, and associates to their advisor.

PART I. Client Education: It's Essential

Each of the advisors feels that client education is critical to a long-term relationship. Each has different preferred approaches to teaching clients about the financial process. The educational process provides clients with the sense of comfort that comes from understanding and appreciating the various processes of the advisory team. Additionally, many advisors feel a personal sense of responsibility to offer their clients additional independence and the self-satisfaction that comes from knowledge.

This is in direct contrast to some lower-level financial salespeople who use the "Trust me. Take my word for it" approach to sell clients whatever product they happen to be pushing. Also be wary of representatives who use a lot of industry jargon and slang. Are they dazzling you with their brilliance or trying to baffle you?

Word to the Wise

If someone says, "Just take my word for it," as a way of avoiding an explanation—don't. A good advisor wants you to be able to make an informed decision. Perhaps the best way to respond to the "just trust me" approach would be to ask whether he or she would mind explaining it to your friend, the (attorney, accountant, venture capitalist, NASD arbitrator, FBI agent, etc). If the financial sales rep avoids or dismisses the question, then you have your answer. On the other hand, if a representative or advisor welcomes the opportunity to share his or her information with another professional, you can feel more comfortable with the idea. His or her willingness to explain something to another professional doesn't necessarily mean the idea is good or appropriate for you; it merely shows that he or she is not trying to hide anything and they believe that the idea will stand up to scrutiny.

Can You Delegate Too Much?

You have a responsibility to yourself to delegate certain tasks, such as money management, to others so that you can make the best use of your time, talents, energy, and interests.

Again, keep in mind that there are certain things in life that you can't delegate. Brian Puckett reminds his clients that they can't delegate actions to enrich their spiritual life. They can't delegate being a better spouse to their husband or wife. And they can't delegate being a better grandparent to their grandchildren."

Therefore, it becomes beneficial to delegate the tasks that can be performed effectively and efficiently by a third party. However, before you delegate you must make sure that you know what you're delegating and that you have a way to evaluate whether or not that task is being properly handled.

One of the easiest ways to evaluate how your financial matters are being handled is to review periodic reports and have periodic meetings with the advisor. Are you achieving your financial goals? Why or why not? Even this type of evaluation requires an investor to have a basic understanding of the financial industry and to know how various parts of their financial or investment plan fit together.

Clients have a personal responsibility to learn about their finances. Hiring a skilled professional to oversee your financial goals is great, but ignorance is not. Here are a few situations where having financial knowledge is useful.

- Too often one spouse takes care of the finances and the other spouse remains in the dark. If the financially oriented spouse dies, the surviving spouse will most likely struggle to understand and take care of financial decisions. In such situations, unless a competent financial advisor is available, there is a high probability that some poor decisions or mistakes will be made. (The same may be applicable for business partners.)
- There is a possibility that the advisor may die and the client may have to find another advisor and team, assuming, for whatever reason, the client doesn't remain with the original team. At that point it would be wise to have a working knowledge of why certain decisions were made so you can relate that information to the new advisory team.
- It may be wise for someone else in the family to understand what's going on in case you become incapacitated.
- You may need to explain the basics of finance and how the estate is structured and funded so that an heir will be able to understand.
- It is helpful to have the know-how to explain finances to your children or friends who come to you for advice. (Remember: Children learn about saving and investing from their parents.)
- Knowing astute questions to ask gives you a decided edge, especially when dealing with financial salespeople who may not have your best interests at heart.

Ultimately, each advisor wants to ensure that clients are making informed decisions and that they understand and are comfortable with the various investment processes the advisor employs.

Bill Baker educates every one of his prospects and clients on the basics of investment management. An example of the education he provides includes the basics of fundamental research, technical research and portfolio risk management. He feels that such education is essential for a good long-term relationship.

Why They Teach

Yale Levey always likes to be a teacher and make a positive impact on people. He says, "I realized not too long ago that I've evolved into being a teacher of sorts—not a classroom teacher, but I am helping and teaching people to avoid mistakes and get what they want out of life." Of course, he concentrates on the financial side, but he is teaching people how to have confidence in their investments or strategies that will enhance their lives.

Cella Quinn's first "classroom" was a local YWCA where she began teaching courses in investments in the mid-1970s. She says that teaching helped her become a "broker's broker" because she had to do quite a bit of research to understand the information in greater depth. She had to learn how to speak English rather than "financialese" so she could explain complex topics to people with different backgrounds and levels of sophistication. Cella says, "When you teach it, you really have to learn it." She continues to speak on a variety of topics, including her current offering "Protect What You Have and Still Retire Before Old Age". It's one of the ways she stays sharp.

Various Approaches to the Educational Process

There are a number of ways that advisors enhance the knowledge and sophistication of their clients. Here are two:

- ***Seminars and Workshops*** are conducted by most advisors in a variety of ways and for various purposes. Public seminars are open to anyone who wishes to attend. They tend to deal with broad topics such as taxation, estate planning, the basics of investing, etc. Many advisors also hold private seminars dealing with topics of specific interest to their clients. These seminars tend to give information in greater depth because the advisor is familiar with the needs and goals of each person attending. Individual meetings with clients are another educational avenue. At those meetings, issues pertinent to the individual client are addressed.

Mark Little started a special kind of client forum after discovering that some of his clients' adult children were going to their parents for advice. Some of those clients were even doing rudimentary financial planning for their children. "So," Mark says, "we created a forum for our clients and their families to do it even better. On one Saturday per month we invite our clients and their family members to learn about various investment topics and to have an open Q&A session."

He usually has a different theme at each meeting and concentrates on that topic for the first hour. During that time people are invited to ask any questions. But, it's the second half that can get really exciting because people can ask questions on any topic, and Mark and his associates provide answers. If some people have questions on 401(k)'s, for example, they'll congregate in a small study group and Mark's chief investment officer will join them. Another person or group might have tax questions, in which case they'll be joined by a CPA.

Mark says those sessions have proven quite productive. The attendees learn about investing and other subjects, and more importantly, those children who sought advice from their parents now get their answers from Mark's professional team.

In contrast, Michael Searcy prefers to provide education in a one-on-one setting where he can explain concepts and issues specific to the client on an as-needed basis. However, he occasionally holds special family workshops or retreats so that the children of clients can get a handle on what is going on in their parents' lives. He and his team also work with families in private family foundation situations so that all of the people responsible for helping designate foundation funds understand the various issues associated with managing the foundation's wealth.

Similarly, Eric Hutchinson ran into a situation in which clients wanted their entire family to understand their estate plan and the reasoning behind some of their decisions. The only problem was that the only time the entire family could get together was at Christmas. So on December 23rd, Eric went to their home and made a presentation on behalf of the parents to the entire family. As he recalls, "It was a wonderful experience to have that conversation with the entire family." Shortly thereafter, Pete (the father) told Eric that when they first started working together he couldn't imagine how Eric was going to be worth his fee. "Now," said Pete, "I'm worried that we're not paying you enough for the kind of value that we're getting."

• ***Written materials*** are available from all advisors and run the gamut from "Introducing Our Team" to advanced tax-planning strategies. Yale Levey maintains a library of information having to do with various types of products and services that they're involved with. Some of the literature is created by product sponsors, some by his broker/dealer. Yale uses it because the information is well done and easy to read. He also has a lot of information on his computer that he can offer clients on most investment topics, such as a list of valuable websites.

Tom Gau is a prolific writer and advisor to other advisors. He's written three booklets entitled *The Top Ten Mistakes People Make When They Inherit an IRA; Is the Beneficiary of Your IRA the IRS?;* and *What You Ought to Know Before You Receive Your Retirement Distributions*. These booklets offer practical ideas on what and what not to do.

Tom offers the following scenario. If someone inherits an IRA it is because he or she is the beneficiary of someone who has just passed away. Assuming there is no surviving spouse, the IRA would, in this example, pass directly to the son or daughter.

The parent "assumes" that the kids will know what to do with it. They probably also "assumed" that the kids would be in a low tax bracket.

When Tom meets one-on-one with the child, he explains that an Inherited IRA is an option available to them that would allow the money to continue growing in a tax-advantaged way. They generally respond, "Thank you, Mr. Gau, for explaining all that to me. However, give me all the money now." Of course, Tom has no choice but to comply.

When counseling someone who currently has a large IRA, Tom will often recommend that an Inherited IRA Trust be the designated beneficiary. It has nearly all the benefits, and helps resolve the problem of letting someone who is not financially astute have immediate access to the funds. Tom knows his clients and their families very well, and when necessary, will suggest that a particular child may not be able to make the smartest decisions when they inherit the money. He then offers his clients alternatives to help protect those children from themselves.

He also mails his booklets and a DVD of a seminar to people who may inherit a large IRA so they have the time to think and learn.

Helping Your Advisor Help You

You can take an active role in seeking education from your advisor by doing the following:

- Let the advisor know about your needs and expectations.
- Ask the advisor to explain any part of the process you don't understand.
- Make sure the advisor communicates on a level that you easily understand.
- Ask the advisor about seminars and other ways to learn more about managing your money.

Questions to Ask Your Advisor

When searching for an advisor, you should ask the candidate to describe his or her last educational event and what topics and material were covered. Also, ask for references of people who have participated in the advisor's educational process.

Special Education Needs

Many advisors work with foundations and pension plans, which means they are in contact with many people who have fiduciary responsibilities. Most people are not well-versed in high finance and in the intricacies of various financial instruments. This, the advisors note, is also true of many trustees who sit on investment committees, foundations, and pension plans. The advisors realize that part of their role in these situations is to provide ongoing education on topics such as:

- Identifying specific, measurable financial objectives and processes
- Portfolio management techniques

- Writing Investment Policy Statements
- Asset allocation, asset classes, asset management
- Roles and services of investment managers
- How to analyze managers and appropriately review quantitative analysis

Essentially, they help teach trustees how to make informed decisions and make education a high priority and an ongoing process.

In Summary

As an investor, you owe it to yourself to continually increase your level of financial understanding. You don't have to be an expert, but you need to know what's going on with your finances. Make sure that any advisor you deal with actively tries to help you increase your level of financial sophistication. An advisor should never use the "black box" approach, meaning they don't reveal any of their investment strategies and tools to you.

As an investor, you have an obligation to you and your family to *learn*. If you are a trustee of any sort, then you also need to research and abide by your fiduciary responsibilities.

Part II. Client Appreciation

All of the advisors show client appreciation in different ways. Some host a yearly event to which all clients are invited; others offer a good dinner at the end of an educational seminar. Another advisor may prefer to meet with clients for a private dinner at a good restaurant. For example, Mike Piershale enjoys offering an annual banquet for all of his clients. In addition, usually at Christmas time, he will rent a movie theater and invite his clients, their kids and grandkids to a private viewing of a good, family movie. The clients get free popcorn and Santa hats. People really enjoy the family atmosphere, the congeniality and Mike's thoughtfulness.

Eric Hutchinson discovered that they could rent the Clinton Presidential Library in Little Rock and arrange for tours for the firm's clients in the evening. "We held a large reception, invited clients to come, had a speaker for them, and they were able to tour the Clinton Library—and do so in private. It was a tremendous event with about 400 clients attending. They absolutely loved it," he says.

The speaker was a physician who is a nationally recognized expert on aging and age-related issues and appropriate for their clientele. Since Hutchinson/Ifrah specializes in retirement planning, they look for speakers who address issues of interest to their clients.

Beyond Seminars and Dinners

Admittedly, client appreciation events are wonderful to attend, but they don't tell the entire story. Appreciation is an attitude that permeates the entire team and shows itself in all the little things that they do for their clients on a regular basis. For instance, George Jackson makes the following comment, "We have the best clients on the planet. We work well with them; we care about them; we have great relationships with them. I just enjoy coming to work and meeting with them. It's just fun. And, it's nice to help them through any difficult situation. It's a very rewarding business."

Here's a small sampling of things we found impressive.

- Craig Pluta and Chris Doughty highlight items of interest about their clients at their client appreciation events. For example, one client is an Associated Press photographer who won an award for his work in Iraq. Another photographer has his work in the London Museum and won a worldwide contest. As Craig says, "We like to do tributes to our clients so that other people can be as inspired by them as we are."
- Both Tom Gau and Mike Piershale give their clients the opportunity to "take a bite out of the IRS" by giving them "Form 1040 chocolate bars."
- When clients visit Tom Gau, they are handed their personalized coffee mug. It's all part of the family atmosphere that he wants to maintain.
- When clients visit Brian Puckett's office, they are greeted with their favorite beverage and, if desired, a snack such as cookies or peanuts.

Appreciation incorporates true caring into the equation. To Brian, it means attending a client's funeral and then spending time with the father and son to discuss what he and his team can do to help.

Appreciation is also a lot of simple things like Cella Quinn's staff letting her know who to send "get well" or other appropriate cards to. It's Bill Baker buying a humorous magazine gift subscription for a client who needed a lift, and it's Craig Pluta discovering that a client was interested in getting involved in woodturning and then sending him a book on woodturning techniques. And it's Page Flanner on the Jackson Retirement Planning team driving 150 miles to help an elderly lady with her taxes—and doing it on her own time.

Appreciation works both ways. Clients often call their advisors to praise the work they've done or to praise a member of the advisory team and the advisor takes the time to relay the message to his or her team member(s). George Jackson says, "All I hear about is how my clients love our team members. I just have a great team." Every other advisor interviewed can echo those sentiments.

In Conclusion

A good advisor is one who cares about your education. A good advisor cares about you and demonstrates that personal interest in your welfare and your life. These people rate a "10" on the Caring Continuum.

◆◆◆

Chapter 16

A Final Word of Advice

Each of the advisors in this book was asked the following question: *If you could give readers one piece of advice on any topic that you think would make the biggest difference, what would that advice be?*

Some of the answers have already been incorporated into the book. We've chosen seven final comments that encapsulate some of the primary points made within these pages. The ideas contain a bit of philosophy, good rules of thumb and a healthy dose of common sense.

We start with a quote from Cella Quinn regarding the need to take a long-term financial view while going through different phases, or passages, of life. It's difficult for most people to keep their eye on the long-term goal of building wealth when going through life's transitions. Her advice is appropriate for people at all stages of life, but is especially important to impart to younger investors.

"Realize that life is a passage and take the long-term view. People go through passages as they age: growing up, getting educated, marrying, having a family, grandchildren. And that's what life's about. Yet throughout all of this, people need to focus on the long-term goal of financial independence. I think the biggest mistake people make is they don't put enough money away for the future and they don't have a long-term outlook with the money they have. Looking at things long-term smoothes out many of life's wrinkles and it makes one a better investor," she says.

Have Clear Goals

One of the keys to having long-term focus is to be clear about who you are, what is important to you, and your goals. Yale Levey says that it's important to be clear about what's important because it will carry through in all aspects of life. He's found that being able to help others create clarity is both a wonderful and powerful thing. Yale says, "If all your advisors are familiar with your goals and you're able to articulate their roles on your team, you are creating one of the best possible teams to help produce optimal results, ensuring you'll meet your specific goals."

He says that you can use the exact same approach in life—with your personal relationships, your spouse, and your friends. If you're very, very clear on what you want, you'll be able to communicate in a more effective manner what it is that you expect.

Yale concludes that people want to be helpful. If they know where they fit and what the expectations are, it's easier for them to succeed. "It's a lot easier to hit the target when you can see it," he says.

Michael Searcy speaks to the issue of clarity and having all advisors work together in a collaborative manner. He cautions against playing, what he calls, "advisor pinball," meaning a client goes to one professional after another, never giving anyone the complete picture. This results in opinions based on partial information. The result is usually a very disjointed financial or investment plan.

Mike says getting together with professionals from different disciplines is a much more effective approach because everyone can contribute ideas and evaluate the ideas of others. Mike says, "For example, I might have an idea that the accountant might like, but he might warn about the tax consequences of one aspect, while the lawyer may discuss the legal implications. The net results from this 'brain trust' are fantastic."

To understand the client's ultimate objectives, Mike and his team spend a lot of time with clients focusing on their visions, what they want to do, and what's most important to them in life.

The Game Plan

Once the objective is determined, a game plan can be created. Advisors will take the information you provide and create a financial or investment plan. Be sure to consider the following critical areas. As Brian Puckett says, some of these are so simple that people overlook them and fail to build them into their plans.

Brian's advice is that you absolutely must have a game plan. As he says,

"Create a comprehensive financial plan to make sure that you and your loved ones enjoy a wonderful life."

Brian offers six critical areas to consider. They are:

1. Have enough money set aside to take care of the inevitable emergency or big market downturn.
2. Ensure against large, predictable, future liabilities like tuition funding for a loved one, or the payment of your mortgage balance. Be able to protect your income stream so that your lifestyle isn't compromised.
3. Make sure that your plan will be accomplished even if you become disabled.
4. Take advantage of various tax strategies.
5. Have a realistic withdrawal rate from your investments. Make sure that you never run out of money.
6. Make sure you've planned for the ever-increasing costs of health care or nursing home care in the event that you, your spouse or your parents need it.

Brian says that if you do all of the above, your wealth is likely to continue to grow. He recommends having a logical, tax-wise estate plan so that your loved ones, not the federal government, receive the benefit of everything you've worked for.

A key component within any financial or investment plan is correctly identifying and managing risk. George Jackson says that most investors don't understand the risk they're taking and, as a result, take on too much. "Often people who have a conservative nature have, unbeknownst to them, a portfolio of high-risk assets. They, therefore, need an objective analysis. The other risk that many people take is getting caught up in the psychology of the crowd. "There's more emotion than logic driving decisions," he says. An advisor's objectivity is important here.

The Right Person for the Job

Finding the right advisor and team to work with is extraordinarily important. They will help you become very clear in your goals, stay the course when times are tough, and monitor your plan and make appropriate adaptations when necessary.

Craig Pluta says that establishing the proper relationship with an advisory team is likely one of the most important relationships you can have because they will be involved with every aspect of finance. Money ultimately affects what you can or cannot do in life.

Chris Doughty adds that you should like the professionals you work with. "You'll be meeting and interacting with your advisor countless times over the years. You want that to be enjoyable. You want to be able to be a team and work together."

The Story of Your Life

Imagine that you have been given the task of writing the screenplay and directing the movie of your life. In addition, you will be the hero of the movie. You will direct the cast of characters—your family—in all of the things (values) you deem important. Of course, you have to write out the basic themes of the story—the themes that detail what you want to leave behind. You'll have to hire some additional production and support people to make sure that the money is there when you want it, that there is documentation to ensure the money goes to the right people in the way you envisioned they should receive it, and others to make sure that the government doesn't take too much of the money. Thus, you'll need a financial advisor, an attorney to draw up the will and trust documents, and an accountant behind the scenes to help you implement your vision. Others may also be needed, depending on how you write the play. You can choose the support team members or hire a casting director.

As the screenwriter and director, you can write the story in whatever genre you please: An adventure, a romance, a comedy, a horror story, or a drama. Is the cast of characters going to be apprised of your wishes before or after your demise? How do you want to interact with them until then? Will they scatter in different directions because of widely diverse, perhaps conflicting, values? Or, will they band together to help future generations to preserve your values, traditions, and wealth?

The questions you have to answer from this day forward are both philosophical and practical. By developing and articulating your vision now, and taking steps – which include using the right people – to ensure that your ideals will be passed on, you have greater assurance that your legacy will not be just your dream, but an important part of the lives of your progeny as well.

In Conclusion

Your financial well-being is of paramount importance. Remember that you are the writer and director of your own story. Your advisory team represents some of the key production people who will help you attain your goals. However, you must choose wisely. You now know what to look for. If you already have a stellar team, let it do the job it was hired to do. If you don't already have a team, all you have learned from this book will assist you in finding a great one.

◆◆◆

A special thanks to the financial advisors for their valuable contributions to this project:

- **William Baker**
Principal and Founder, William Baker & Associates, Inc.
Investment Management and Financial Planning Specialists
400 Galleria Parkway Ste 1500; Atlanta, GA 30339
Telephone: 770-956-4073 Email: bbaker@wmbaker.com
Website: www.wmbakerinvest.com
Securities offered and supervised by Wilbanks Securities,Inc. Member NASD/SIPC/MSRB; 4334 NW Expwy, Suite 222, Oklahoma City,OK 73116 405-842-0202; Fee based through Wilbanks Securities Advisory

- **Chris Doughty**
Co-Founder of the ReAct! Group
First Vice President Ziegler Investments Services Group
250 E Wisconsin Ave., 20th Fl; Milwaukee, WI 53202
Telephone: 414-978-6521 Email: cdoughty@ziegler.com

- **Thomas B. Gau, CPA, CFP®, MBA, CRIA,**
Principal, Oregon Pacific Financial Advisors, Inc.
645 A Street, Ashland, OR 97520
Telephone: (541) 482-0138 Email: tom@opfa2.com

- **Eric Hutchinson, CFP®**
Chairman & CEO, Hutchinson/Ifrah Financial Services, Inc
12511 Cantrell Road; Little Rock, AR 72223
Telephone: 501-223-9190 Email: eric@hutchinson-ifrah.com

- **George P. Jackson, MBA, CPA*, CFA, CFP®, CLU, ChFC**
President, Jackson Retirement Planning, Inc.
1515 International Pkwy, Ste 1013; Heathrow, FL 32746
Telephone: 407-834-4322 Email: george@jacksonretirement.com
Website: www.JacksonRetirement.com
*Regulated by the state of Florida

- **Yale Levey, CFP®[1]**
Managing Director, Roseland Financial Group, LLC
Managing Executive, Royal Alliance Associates Inc.[2]
101 Eisenhower Parkway, Box C; Roseland, NJ 07068
Telephone: 973-228-6566 Email: yale@roselandfinancialgroup.com
Website: www.advisorsinphilanthropy.org

[1] Chartered Advisor in Philanthropy Candidate
[1] Member International Association Advisors in Philanthropy
[2]Securities offered through Royal Alliance Associates, Inc., member NASD/SIPC

- **Mark Little**
Founder and Creator, The Freedom Experience®
2313 Lockhill Selma, Ste 221; San Antonio, Texas 78230
Telephone: 888-467-8593 Email: mark@thefreedomexperience.com

- **Mike Piershale**
Registered Principal, Raymond James Financial Services, Inc.
4318 W. Crystal Lake Road, Unit H; McHenry, IL 60050
Telephone: 815-363-3368 Email: Mike.Piershale@raymondjames.com

- **Craig Pluta**
Co-Founder, The ReAct! Group
First Vice President, Zeigler Investment Services Group
250 E Wisconsin Ave., 20th Fl; Milwaukee, WI 53202
Telephone: 414-978-6520 Email: cpluta@ziegler.com

- **Brian W. Puckett, JD, CPA/PFS**
Brian Puckett Retirement Advisors, LLC[1]
9400 N. Broadway Extension, Ste 540;
Oklahoma City, OK 73114
Telephone: 405-607-4820 or 800-401-6477
Email: info@puckettadvisors.com Website: www.puckettadvisors.com

[1] Securities and Investment Advisory Services offered through Cambridge Investment Research, Inc., a registered Broker/Dealer, Member NASD/SIPC, and a federally registered investment advisor. Cambridge Investment Research, Inc. and Brian Puckett Retirement Advisors, LLC are not affiliated companies. The Smart Choice for Your Quality of Life.

- **Cella Quinn**
President and CEO, Cella Quinn Investment Services[1]
10908 Forrest Drive Omaha NE 68144
Telephone: 402-392-2111 or 800-772-1160
Email: cellaquinn@cellaquinn.com Website: www.cellaquinn.com

[1] Securities offered through ADVANTAGE CAPITAL CORPORATION. A Registered Broker/Dealer, NASD/SIPC

- **Michael J. Searcy, ChFC, CFP®, AIF®**
President, Searcy Financial Services, Inc.
13220 Metcalf Avenue, Ste 360; Overland Park, KS 66213
Telephone: 913-814-3800 Email: mike@searcyfinancial.com
Website: www.searcyfinancial.com